CATHOLIC SPIRITUALITY IN FOCUS

CATHOLIC SPIRITUALITY IN FOCUS
Eight Themes of Mind and Heart

George E. Saint-Laurent, S.T.D.

First Edition 2007

Published in the United States by
Paragon House
1925 Oakcrest Avenue, Suite 7
St. Paul, MN 55113

Biblical quotations were all taken from:
The New Oxford Annotated Bible with the Apocrypha. Metzger, Bruce M. & Roland Murphy, Eds. New York: Oxford University Press, 1991.

Library of Congress Cataloging-in-Publication Data

Saint-Laurent, George E.
  Catholic spirituality in focus : eight themes of mind and heart / George E. Saint-Laurent. -- 1st ed.
      p. cm.
  Summary: "A manual for Catholic life and practice based on discipleship to Christ within the Church"--Provided by publisher.
  Includes bibliographical references.
  ISBN 1-55778-865-0 (alk. paper)
  1. Spirituality--Catholic Church. 2. Christian life--Catholic authors. I. Title.
  BX2350.65.S24 2007
  248.4'82--dc22

                              2006037414

Manufactured in the United States of America
10 9 8 7 6 5 4 3 2 1

The paper used in this publication meets the minimum requirements of American National Standard for Information Sciences—Permanence of Paper for Printed Library Materials, ANSIZ39.48-1984.

For current information about all releases from Paragon House,
visit the web site at http://www.paragonhouse.com

I dedicate this book to three remarkable women of spiritual depth who are at once my dear family and my best friends: my beloved wife, Michaeleen Saint-Laurent, and my two wonderful daughters, Marie-Louise and Jeanne-Nicole. By your loving example, you have taught me more about Catholic spirituality than I have ever learned from books.

CONTENTS

Chapter Four   51

CHRISTIAN VALUES
A Prophetic Model of Christian Values: Jacques Maritain

Chapter Five   67

CHRISTIAN VOLITION
A Prophetic Model of Christian Volition: Joan Chittester

Chapter Six   83

CHRISTIAN VITALITY
A Prophetic Model of Christian Vitality:
Dr. Albert Schweitzer

Chapter Seven   101

CHRISTIAN VIRTUE
A Prophetic Model of Christian Virtue:
Mother Teresa of Calcutta

Chapter Eight   119

CHRISTIAN VOYAGE
A Prophetic Model of Christian Voyage:
St. Augustine of Hippo

INTRODUCTION

Each of the world's scriptured religions proposes an enlightened or "revealed" vision of reality. Each of them offers a sacred worldview, that is, a total perspective that unifies all things material and spiritual, giving them coherent meaning in relationship to the Absolute and the Holy. Such a cosmic window provides a subliminal lens for penetrating the vast universe about us, yet each of them fosters a heightened consciousness of the even deeper mystery within us. Each of the world's religions understands the meaning of human life in terms of a "glad tidings" of salvation, and most of them are happy to invite others to share in their religious commitment: "Come and see if you can see what we have seen for our joy."

Each sacred vision springs from a tradition that includes, promotes, and nurtures religious *spirituality* not as a contrast, but as its own proper fruit. Indeed, every scriptured religion claims the spiritual enrichment of its adherents as its principal concern. Yet each tradition is far more complete and comprehensive than spirituality alone, including (as it unfailingly does) its special sources of spirituality: a developed belief system, a structured order of ritual and cult, and a practical guide for ethical life.

Over the centuries, practitioners of these religions have persuaded millions of people to embrace some particular perspective as their own and to order their lives accordingly. According to these traditions, for example, we are all in grave trouble (variously interpreted as "sin," "error," or "illusion"), but compelling reasons validate their saving path to forgiveness from sin or illumination from error. There is *more* to reality, they all insist, than our perceived world of the senses. We can surpass this physical world and find ultimate fulfillment in that *more*, a transcendent Something or Someone.

Historical, cultural, and theological development is, of course, inevitable within all the religions. Most of them insist, nevertheless, upon the original simplicity of their worldview, a foundational wisdom that retains its purity despite generations of accretions and structural complexities. We can categorize most of these sacred visions in terms of three dimensions: a charismatic master of supernal wisdom, a privileged "way" proclaimed by that teacher, and an institutionalized community that looks back to him.

For example, Buddhists, who are nontheists, "take refuge" in (1) Siddhartha Gautama, the Buddha, (2) the Middle Way of the Buddha's *Dharma* ("saving teaching"), and (3) the *Sangha* ("monastic order"). Among monotheistic religions, on the other hand, Jews pursue a holy life according to (1) Moses, Israel's premier teacher, (2) the Way of *Torah* ("teaching"), and (3) the gathering of the

K'lal Yisrael ("Catholic Israel"). Muslims strive for fidelity as God's servants in terms of (1) Muhammad, the seal of the prophets, (2) observance of the "straight path" of the *Quran*, and (3) the unity of the Islamic *Umma* ("nation"). Christians believe in a divine adoption as God's children in terms of (1) Jesus the Christ, who is Lord and Savior, (2) following the way of Christ's Gospel, and (3) a communal life in Christ's holy Church.

Our Christian experience unfolds in terms of a personal relationship with Christ. It is fundamentally a matter of allowing God's Holy Spirit to clothe us as new creatures in Christ—with Christ's mind, his heart, his hands, and his feet. Within the Christian family, we Catholics (and also Orthodox Christians) insist further upon the ecclesial dimension of our Christ-life: We always experience our Christian spirituality communally, with and through the holy Church.

It is Christ who calls us in our *vocation* to become his disciples. Then we must look out upon the world with Christ's *vision;* we must address God and one another with Christ's *voice.* In our discipleship, we must learn to determine our options in terms of Christ's *value*s, to commit ourselves in fidelity by Christ's *volition*, to live by Christ's *vitality*, to guide our freedom by Christ's *virtue*, and to share in Christ's *voyage* to the Father.

We can understand our spirituality as living consciously within the embrace of God's unconditional love.

Christ has proclaimed the Good News that God is essentially Love *(Agape)*. Our God is unconditional Love in a trinity of relationships as God the Father (the Lover), God the Son (the Loved), and God the Holy Spirit (the Love). Our God is everlasting Love in boundless justice, mercy, power, and wisdom. God the Father incarnated the divine love in Jesus, who demonstrated God's love conclusively by his Cross and Resurrection *(Paschal Mystery)*. Christ established his holy Church as a communion of love in his Holy Spirit, and Christ actively pours forth his Spirit of love upon all his members by Word and Sacrament.

Catholic spirituality springs from a dynamic faith, a personal engagement with Christ as the human embodiment of divine love. Catholic spirituality finds its stability in an unshakable hope, a trust in the Risen Christ as the victory of God's love over sin and death. Catholic spirituality finds its fulfillment in a powerful love for God and for all our brothers and sisters by Christ's Holy Spirit.

Catholics who are intent upon nurturing their spirituality must realize that they are entering into a process of open-ended development. Christian spirituality is a walk with Christ, a journey of gradual growth toward a maturity that beckons them ever again from up ahead, and there are no recesses or vacations. Deeper spirituality demands that we be ready daily to advance one more step with generosity and confront one more vicissitude with courage.

Richer spirituality requires much more than regular

sacramental practice and faithful observance of ecclesiastical law. We begin our journey as disciples intent upon following Christ, but we must persevere as friends gifted with life in Christ. Daily we must deny ourselves and give ourselves over from merely notional faith to real faith—from external adherence to a personal involvement with Christ that reaches down to our bones, courses through our arteries, and underlies all our consciousness.

We must grow from an intellectualized faith—an understanding that is theologically orthodox, perhaps, but cold, cerebral, and ineffectual—to a wisdom born of love. We must mature from superficial joy in delightful stories into a life-changing conviction, from mere wonder at miraculous events into eucharistic worship for the praise of the glory of Christ's grace, from verbal confession of the Creed to an unreserved commitment with all our being. We must advance beyond inspiring cognitions about Christ to the surpassing knowledge of Christ himself and his love. We can achieve this remarkable goal through reflective prayer in private, liturgical celebration with the community, and the loving service of others.

As we focus upon Catholic spirituality, we shall explore eight of its constituent dimensions one by one: vocation, vision, voice, values, volition, vitality, virtue, and voyage. Yet we must retain our appreciation of Catholic spirituality in all its wholeness, a single mystery of grace beyond rational analysis and theological categories. Catholic spirituality is *all about* believing in God's love and living consciously within its embrace; the rest is detail.

Chapter One

CHRISTIAN VOCATION

*"This is my commandment: love one another as I have
loved you. There is no greater love than this: to lay
down one's life for one's friends. You are my friends if
you do what I command you. I no longer speak of you
as slaves, for a slave does not know what his master
is about. Instead, I call you friends, since I have made
known to you all that I heard from my Father. It was
not you who chose me, it was I who chose you to go forth
and bear fruit."* (John 15:12—16a)

A PROPHETIC MODEL OF CHRISTIAN VOCATION: GODFREY DIEKMANN, O.S.B.

My family's initial glimpse of him occurred upon
our arrival for Sunday Mass at the great chapel of
St. John's Abbey in Collegeville, Minnesota. Since this grand
old priest could no longer join in with the solemn proces-
sion down the main aisle, he had seated himself beforehand
in the second choir stall to the left of the sanctuary. "There
he is!" I exclaimed in an excited whisper to Michaeleen
and my daughters Marie-Louise and Jeanne-Nicole. "That
white-haired man at prayer is the great Father Godfrey

Diekmann!" Over the following semester of our stay at the abbey's Ecumenical Center, each of us would come to know, love, and revere this remarkable Benedictine monk. We felt a deeply personal loss when we heard of his final passage into the joyful peace of everlasting life in heaven.

Father Godfrey was an energetic servant of God, a faithful friend of Christ, and a grateful son of the Church. He was a liturgical scholar, a sacramental theologian, an eloquent preacher, a prolific author, and much, much more. Some of us may recall certain "holy" people as being cold and distant, forbidding and judgmental—even fearsome. But Father Godfrey Diekmann was a person of immense personal charm and charisma, someone whom my family and I shall always remember as a person loving both of God and of people, guileless and uncomplicated.

I found one of Father Godfrey's most attractive traits to be his childlike innocence seasoned with quick wit. (He confessed that his only claim to fame was never to have eaten in a McDonald's restaurant!) Godfrey thoroughly enjoyed good conversation in company with his friends. He also liked to surprise them with small gifts such as a souvenir photograph of himself or a loaf of freshly baked "Johnny bread." Once he picked some wild watercress, washed and packaged it, and then left it outside our door. We were delighted, of course, with the greens, but so grateful for the affection that inspired his giving.

Godfrey Diekmann embodied the famous aphorism

of St. Irenaeus of Lyon: "The glory of God is a human being fully alive!" Father Diekmann, the monk, could share his passion for the spiritual renewal of the Church, yet Godfrey, the man, could exult in the simple things of life (he took modest pride in his special recipe for making fresh pesto sauce). Father Diekmann, the professional liturgiologist, could delight in scholarly research of Ethiopic manuscripts, yet Godfrey, the amateur naturalist, loved to explore the monastery woods—he once discovered a mushroom previously unlisted in the botanical books.

Father Godfrey lived out the Benedictine axiom *ora et labora* ("pray and work"). He was a true contemplative and probably a mystic in his order's tradition of *lectio divina* ("divine reading"), yet he was vulnerably accessible to people. When we visited Godfrey one last time before departing for our home in California, I asked him to give us his priestly blessing. After granting my request, the great Godfrey Diekmann knelt at my feet and asked for my blessing in turn! I was overwhelmed by his gracious humility.

During his long life, Father Godfrey made an enormous contribution to the Church that he loved. He was a leader among the international scholars working for liturgical renewal. He edited and contributed regularly to an influential journal known first as *Orate Fratres* and later as *Worship*. He taught Patristics to seminarians and conducted retreats for religious, clerics, and laypeople. He presented lectures and keynote addresses before national conferences.

He was a monk's monk, a priest's priest, and a believer's believer.

In so many ways, Father Godfrey made a decisive and far-reaching impact upon the spirituality of American Catholics, a contribution that will extend for many generations to come. For Father Godfrey was an uncommonly affable human being who had answered wholeheartedly Christ's call to Christian discipleship.

Godfrey gave himself generously to the Benedictine vocation that determined his monastic state of life within the Church. He responded unreservedly to the clerical vocation that appointed him to priestly service within the Church. Throughout his life, however, Father Godfrey committed himself to one vocation above all: his call to Christian discipleship.

The Theme of Christian Vocation

Catholic spirituality stems from the Christian *vocation*, and our Christian vocation originates in Jesus Christ, the risen Master. Christ calls each of us individually to follow him in his holy Church, and Christ's love of predilection initiates a lifetime of special friendship. Our vocation gives us our truest identity as disciples of our Lord. For we become persons individually known, persons mercifully forgiven, persons uniquely gifted, persons who are made to know that we are wondrously, gratuitously loved.

To be called by Christ makes us privileged persons indeed, but it does not make us superior to others; rather, our vocation makes us more accountable to God as witnesses to others. (By the same token, the Jews realize that as God's chosen people they bear a grave responsibility to reflect God's holiness.) Our Christian calling constitutes us as people of faith, hope, and love. Our vocation expands our lives with purpose and meaning; it energizes our practice in the apostolate and it validates our assemblies for worship. Christ summons us, and we must find nourishment within our holy Tradition and support within our Communion of Saints.

As called persons, we do not depend ultimately upon eloquent preaching, Bible study, or theological formation for our vision, although the stories about Jesus surely enlighten our minds. We do not require rigorous asceticism, lengthy prayers, or moral rectitude for our worldview, although the lifestyle of Jesus wholly inspires our hearts. We do not even need beautiful rituals, monumental art, or lofty cathedrals for our context, although incarnationalism and sacramentalism deeply nourish our spirits. We must ultimately belong to the Risen Christ who calls us to be his disciples; we must come to *know* him who surpasses all knowledge.

In his Resurrection, Jesus became the firstborn of a New Creation. He became the Lord who has received all authority in heaven and earth. He could see all humankind being graced as children of God, the totality of human relationships being deepened in a community of love, and the entire cosmos being transfigured in the refulgent splendor of his light. Christ's final words to his disciples were a solemn commission that they should preach his Gospel to every person and to every nation. Today Christ calls each of us also to be his disciples for ministry and mission.

Because of Christ, God is re-creating all things within a new heaven and a new earth. With Christ, God has graciously redeemed us, and God gathers us to God's self. In Christ, God has mercifully saved us for everlasting happiness in the world to come. Through Christ, God has poured forth God's Holy Spirit to renew the face of the earth. It is, therefore, Jesus Christ who personally calls each of us to live in his Spirit.

Within Christ's holy Church, moreover, we nurture a spirituality fully Christian and distinctively Catholic. For us, sanctification is a process, and salvation is a goal still to be won. We must daily meet challenges old and new along our lifelong pilgrimage. Our Christian life is a mystery; God's grace gently interacts with our personal freedom. Our spirituality demands constant renewal; sometimes we progress forward, but at other times we fall short and we must rise again. We have been called and we have responded, yet we must always acknowledge our sinfulness and seek forgiveness once again. Our spirituality requires constancy of trust despite our infidelities, since Christ's loving call to us endures insistently on a daily basis.

Our spirituality, therefore, always and everywhere centers upon Jesus Christ, who gently and repeatedly invites us to Christian discipleship in his holy Church. The way of discipleship to which Christ calls us can be harsh and demanding. Whatever our difficulties, however, our Catholic spirituality can give us a sense of meaningful purpose through them all.

Even our disabilities can be a positive blessing in disguise. We may experience bodily weakness, but that may occasion a humility that reduces our inflated egos down to size. We may feel the weight of illness, but we may for that reason strengthen our resolve to overcome anxieties. We may endure excruciating pain, but we may consequently become compassionate toward suffering people whom we previously had not noticed. We may become dependent upon the caring service of others, but we may therefore foster a more loving heart. We may become immobilized, flat on our back in bed and out of commission physically, but that may lead to prayerful reflection and more conscious communion with God.

In this chapter, we shall consider our Christian vocation from three perspectives: (1) our call to discipleship in community, (2) our personal relationship with Christ, and (3) our community of the called.

Our Call to Discipleship in Community
The Catholic tradition has always produced spiritual lumi-

naries—women and men who have shared their graced insights into the Christian life. St. Anthony of the Desert and St. Hildegard of Bingen, St. Francis of Assisi and St. Therese of Lisieux, St. Thomas More and St. Theresa of Avila may come to mind out of a vast multitude of saints who have enriched our heritage. Yet the weighty counsels of these saints would be fanciful and hollow, had they not first realized Jesus' call to discipleship in community.

Catholicism has also endorsed various schools of spiritual growth, whose approach has suited diverse temperaments, aptitudes, and cultural milieus. There are, for example, the Benedictines with their balance of liturgical prayer and work, the Franciscans with their emphasis upon simplicity and poverty, and the Jesuits with their fidelity to the *Spiritual Exercises*. Each of these "schools" has had its enthusiastic advocates, and each of them has made a substantive contribution to our holy Tradition. Yet none of these schools would be authentically Catholic were they not rooted in our basic vocation to Christian discipleship in community.

Catholicism distinguishes several "vocations" according to various states in life. Thus there are the sacramental vocations to marriage and to the ordained priesthood, the calling to the single life in the world and to the consecrated ("religious") life. Yet all these particular callings would be meaningless if they did not spring from our fundamental vocation to discipleship in community. All of us in our baptism receive the universal call to sanctity within the holy Church.

Catholicism also recognizes multiple "vocations" according to ministerial gifts for service in the Church. Those with the gifts of teaching and preaching, for example, interpret their proficiency in speaking as an invitation to proclaim God's Word before the worshiping assembly. Similarly, various persons acknowledge their particular talents as empowerments for manual craftsmanship, music and artistic creativity, pastoral leadership, healing, writing, prophecy, conflict resolution, leadership, counseling, visitation of the sick and imprisoned, and the rest. All of these gifts serve to build up the Body of Christ. Yet each of them is a specification of our more fundamental vocation to Christian discipleship in community.

Our vocation to discipleship in community is a call to assume the "discipline" of Jesus, our teacher. But we need not understand "discipline" as some heavy, negative burden, just as we need not interpret "education" as a harsh and punishing regimen. An etymological note can be helpful here. Our English word "disciple" actually comes from the Latin words *discere*, "to learn," and *discipere*, "to comprehend." By the same token, our word "discipline" derives from the Latin *disciplina*, "teaching" or "training." A Christian disciple, then, is one who has entered into a learning process, the training of Christ.

Our Personal Relationship with Christ

Our vocation becomes the point of departure for growth

into a personal relationship with Christ. Jesus, the Risen Christ, alive and available as Son-of-God-in-power, takes the initiative and summons each of us by name at our baptism. Now, at this moment of salvation history, and here, in this particular place within the redeemed world, the Risen Christ addresses each of us with a personalized invitation: "(Elizabeth…Philip…Margaret…Richard), I love you; come, follow me."

Our Lord fixes his eyes upon each of us and graciously waits upon our freedom. Some of us hear his voice in adult baptism, and we respond deliberately and accountably. Most of us "hear" our calling in infant baptism, and our godparents respond on our behalf. Whatever our individual circumstances, however, each of us upon reaching our maturity must make our own responsible commitment, and nobody else may serve as our proxy. We then appropriate our vocation as our truest interior identity.

Jesus is gloriously alive and, therefore, he addresses us in the present. This is a matter of existential fact and not of some pious fantasy. Jesus is risen to new life. That he should know each of us individually from our mother's womb is a matter of liberating truth and not of some wishful indulgence. Jesus is exalted Lord. That he should love each of us personally from the first moment of our conception is a matter of saving reality and not of some poetic hyperbole.

Christ possesses each one of us, and he will neither give up on us nor let us go. Personal relationships depend upon mutual knowledge and recognition, and Christ gives each one of us a place of privilege in his attention. It is for us to fasten our attention upon him by committed faith. Personal relationships rest upon mutual love and concern, and Christ grants each one of us a place of priority within his intention. It is for us to reciprocate and fasten our intention upon him by steadfast hope and faithful love. Personal relationships require mutual communication and dialogue, and Christ speaks to us one-on-one. It is for us to maintain our conversation with active communion of mind and heart.

We, then, have not chosen Christ, but Christ has first chosen us. Since we could not contact Christ, he has first reached out to us and created a lasting relationship with himself. Christ reveals his unconditional love for us, empowering us not only to know and love him in return but also to love others as he has loved us. Christ unites us to himself in a bond of unimaginable connectedness, endurance, and power. Our greatest saints have recognized this priceless friendship, and they have responded with joy and thanksgiving.

Christ's personal relationship with us is not a once-and-for-all-event, but an ongoing work in progress. It is a saving communion that deepens throughout our mortal lives. We are pilgrims-on-the-way, disciples-in-the-making. St. Ignatius of Antioch felt that he would not become a complete disciple until he finally endured death by bloody martyrdom for Christ. Jesus has invited us to embark upon an arduous voyage, and we can expect fierce storms, tumultuous waves, and even perhaps "second planks" after shipwreck. Yet we must persevere through it all by Christ's grace.

Christ challenges us not only to die to selfishness but also to rise in new life with him. He empowers us daily to pass over through all our deaths of mind, body, and spirit in order to enter into new and restored life. Our Lord does not leave us vulnerably alone, but remains within us to accompany us and enliven us.

In Catholic spirituality, we see our vocation as imitating Christ. Christ is, indeed, our supreme exemplar, and we want to be much more like him. We recognize the sanctity of our great heroines and heroes in terms of their Christlike lives. We work to assume the vision of Christ's mind and the values of his heart. We strive to emulate Christ's integrity and fidelity in our own moral lives. We seek to become what Jesus was: courageously humble and selflessly loving.

But this "imitation" is not a superficial modeling of our lives after a distant Christ who reigns gloriously from above, although he is exalted in heaven. Nor is it merely an external walking in the footsteps of a Christ who leads from up in front, although he has, indeed, gone before us and shown us the way. Our Christian discipline of imitating Christ is a matter of dwelling *in* him who possesses us.

Our Lord has come that we may have more abundant life within a personal relationship. He calls us to become a new being in himself, within a mutual inter-indwelling. Christ is the true Bread, and we consume his Flesh and Blood; so we abide in him and he abides in us. Christ is the true Vine and we are the branches, so we remain in him and he remains in us. Christ is the true Light and we are the lamps, so we let our light shine before women and men. Our ever-deeper realization of this saving truth sustains our joy and fortifies our hope.

Still, our vocation to Christian discipleship involves much more. When Christ lives within us, he shares his divine Sonship with us. He pours forth his Holy Spirit upon us to transform us into God's children. Christ is the natural Son of God, and we share by grace in that divine Sonship as God's adoptive children. We enjoy a wondrous rebirth at our baptism so that we are born of God, sons and daughters in the Son. That is why we are privileged affectionately to address God as Jesus himself did: "*Abba* ("Daddy"), dear Father!" That is why we are emboldened to pray: "Our Father, who art in heaven, hallowed be thy Name...."

Our Community of the Called

Most of the great religions stress community; for example, Muslims belong to the Islamic *Umma*, while Buddhists belong to the Buddhist *Sangha*. The Jews belong to God's Covenanted People, and they understand that they will realize God's promises only through, with, and in the holy community. As Christian disciples in the Catholic tradition, we receive the call to enter God's own people in Christ, and we anticipate God's promises only through, with, and in the holy Church.

Some people nowadays protest that they are "very spiritual," but they have no need for "religion." Sometimes the very word *religion* reminds them of negative experiences from their personal history. The fullness of Catholic spirituality, however, is necessarily connected with participation in Christ's Church. Our religious practices need not be burdensome, mechanical, or ritualistic, but fulfilling.

Other people suggest that they do not need any church, since they can "lead a good life" by themselves. And we might well agree with them, were Christianity no more than an ethical method. We often have agnostic or atheistic friends who inspire us by their integrity and shame us by their selflessness. They neither pray nor worship nor make any place for God in their lives, yet they are admirably decent and compassionately humanitarian. We believe, nevertheless, that membership in Christ's Church is not merely an aid to moral life, but is rather a life of grace as God's adopted children.

Some people even argue that they want to follow Christ, but they oppose institutional Christianity with its clerical structures and regulations. We, however, understand our vocation to Christian discipleship not only as personal, but also as communal and ecclesial. The Church's ordained minister voices this calling on the occasion of sacramental baptism. We gather together communally at the altar and celebrate the Holy Eucharist in memory of Christ; our pinnacle experience as Catholics is an ecclesial event within which we realize our truest identity.

Our vocation to follow Jesus as our Teacher, Lord, and Savior achieves its complete extension and depth within his Church. Our gift of faith discovers its fullest expanse within communal celebration together with confession of Christ and service of others. We cannot unite with Christ apart from our brothers and sisters who also belong to him; we cannot persevere on our journey with Christ without the support of our fellow-pilgrims who pursue the same path. (It is no accident that the original meaning of our word "Church" was the "assembly of the called ones"—in Latin, *Ecclesia*, in Greek, *Ekklesia*.)

> *But you are a chosen race, a royal priesthood, a holy nation, God's own people, in order that you may proclaim the mighty acts of him who called you out of darkness into his marvelous light. Once you were not a people, but now you are God's people; once you had not received mercy, but now you have received mercy.* (1 Peter 2:9–10)

Toward Reflective Journaling

Faithful discipleship according to Christ's mind and heart requires that I respond daily to Our Lord's loving call and to the unique offer of his friendship.

QUESTIONS FOR DISCUSSION

1. Can you discern your personal vocation to be a disciple of Jesus Christ in his holy Church?

2. Can you distinguish Christ's commission that you give of yourself and your gifts in service to others?

Chapter Two

CHRISTIAN VISION

When the book of the prophet Isaiah was handed him, he unrolled the scroll and found the passage where it was written: "The spirit of the Lord is upon me; therefore he has anointed me. He has sent me to bring glad tidings to the poor, to proclaim liberty to captives, recovery of sight to the blind and release to prisoners, to announce a year of favor from the Lord." Rolling up the scroll he gave it back to the assistant and sat down. All in the synagogue had their eyes fixed on him. Then he began by saying to them, "This day this Scripture passage is fulfilled in your hearing." (Luke 4:17–21)

A PROPHETIC MODEL OF CHRISTIAN VISION: DOROTHY DAY

I found it difficult to make dinner conversation with this remarkable gray-haired woman seated on my right. She was not arrogant or intimidating; in fact, she was simply spoken and plainly dressed, of humble and retiring manner, of gentle bearing that softened her decisiveness. I could sense the depths of her compassionate love shining through her penetrating gaze, and I was awed by her charisma. Here was truly a woman of God!

I could scarcely believe that I had been able to arrange for this noble woman to speak in my lecture series. Yet here she was, actually present beside me: Dorothy Day, perhaps the most admired woman among contemporary Catholics and surely one of America's premier saints. Dorothy had long been a personal heroine for both Michaeleen and myself, and we had admired her from a distance. The name "Dorothy Day" had always been first on our lips when we recalled contemporary women who exemplified the Gospel. Now she was sitting here beside me at the table, and I was trying desperately to make my banal observations to a woman of uncommon depth.

"Isn't it a shame, Dorothy," I ventured, "to see how San Francisco has become so dangerous? Tourists used to be able to walk fearlessly about 'The City' and enjoy themselves."

"George," Dorothy rejoined, "we cannot be afraid." "Of course," I answered weakly, "we cannot be afraid. No. But isn't it a pity that people are no longer free to walk the streets late at night?"

"George," Dorothy repeated firmly, "we cannot be afraid."

"You are right, Dorothy," I allowed again, "we must not be afraid. But wouldn't we be foolish to visit the Tenderloin in the wee hours of the morning?"

"But George," Dorothy said, fixing her clear eyes unflinchingly upon me, "we cannot be afraid." I was reduced to silence. What could I say? Dorothy Day understood that Christ had commanded us not to fear, and that was that. I have seldom felt so dumb.

Months later, I saw a photograph of policemen in full riot gear approaching the octogenarian Dorothy Day in Delano, California. She had come to support Cesar Chavez and his United Farm Workers. Her face was remarkably calm and tranquil but also unintimidated, as she sat on the sidewalk, staring down these rather overbearing representatives of law and order. Dorothy had been jailed for civil disobedience many times in her life, and she was not about to become frightened now by any threat of force.

Dorothy Day's spirituality was at once determinedly Catholic, faithfully evangelical, and prophetic for all seasons. She believed that Christ's vision was unequivocal in its meaning and nonnegotiable in its demands, so she devoted all she had to its pursuit. Dorothy Day had already been a social radical before her adult conversion to the Church, but now she became a radical Catholic, deeply rooted in Christ and in his Good News for the poor.

Dorothy collaborated with her friend Peter Maurin in founding the Catholic Worker movement with its houses of hospitality for the lonely, the destitute, and the hopeless. A gifted journalist, she also founded and edited *the Catholic Worker* newspaper, for which she wrote provocative articles about Christ's call for social justice.

Dorothy worked tirelessly for the outcasts and the

marginalized, the "winos" and the drug addicts, because Jesus had felt special concern for the desperate. She fed the hungry, clothed the naked, and sheltered the homeless, because Jesus had made service of the needy a condition for entering heaven. Occasionally Dorothy had to conquer her natural revulsion and clean the stinking toilets of the sick, but she understood that in ministering to others she was serving Jesus.

Dorothy Day embraced the Christian vision, and so she discovered her life's meaning in her total self-gift to others. She became an irrepressible advocate for the vulnerable and the defenseless. She combined her passion for peace and social justice with an untiring ministry to individual persons. She worked humbly and shunned the limelight, but she demonstrated for all the world what extraordinary impact a single individual can make.

Dorothy Day cried out against violence in every form, whether martial or systemic, whether economic or social. She devoted all her time and gifts to promoting a personalist world of justice and love. Dorothy put her body on the line in demonstrating for peace, and she stood up openly for oppressed workers on strike. She suffered imprisonment for civil disobedience, because she would not waver in her fidelity to the Gospel.

Most of all, Dorothy devoted herself to the difficult and exacting task of loving people disinterestedly, seeking no return. She could write from experience, "We have all known the long loneliness and we have learned that the only solution is love and that love comes with community." No one would suggest that Dorothy Day was "sweet" or "pretty" like the saints in dreams, but she was a saintly person of "harsh and terrible love." She was real and authentic; what you saw was what you got, with no frills and no sentimental piety.

Catholics are insistently incarnational. In every age and place we need someone like Dorothy Day, who dedicates herself to realizing all that the Gospel promises. My generation is privileged to have known this remarkable woman who made the Christian vision the light of her mind, the passion of her heart, and, therefore, the work of her hands.

The Theme of Christian Vision

Our Catholic spirituality flows from Christian *vision*, and our vision draws upon the Gospel of Christ. Our Lord is our Way, our Truth, and our Life; thus our vision is at once humanistic and supernatural, realistic and idealistic. We see the contemporary situation of humankind Christocentrically and Christologically, not only as it is now but also as it will be in the New Heaven and the New Earth. We interpret the world not only in its present brokenness, misery, and death, but also in its wondrous potential for future healing and transformation by Christ's Spirit.

In this chapter we shall consider our Catholic vision from three perspectives: (1) Christ, our focal point, (2) Christ, our horizon, and (3) our Catholic worldview.

Christ, Our Focal Point

The focal point of our vision is the very person of Christ himself in his exaltation. Indeed, the enduring significance of our Christian story radiates outward from the Risen Christ and refers back to the Risen Christ. Catholic spirituality must be unexceptionally and always Christocentric, since our religious life within the Church revolves about a personal relationship with Jesus of Nazareth, now revealed as mediator, high priest, and Lord of salvation.

Over the course of two thousand years, Catholicism has been subject to institutional corruption and clerical oppression, externalistic and hypocritical observance, legalism and extremism, and displaced priorities with misplaced emphases. Catholic spirituality itself can be extremely complex in its concrete forms, overladen with cultural accretions and "little traditions." Some would argue that Catholicism has appropriated much that is superficial, tangential, and alien to the Gospel. Through and despite it all, however, Catholic spirituality has remained solidly grounded in the Risen Christ. Our Lord continues to hold unrivaled primacy at the center of our vision.

Christ is not, after all, just one great religious teacher among many others who have imparted wisdom, gathered a community of disciples, and then passed on to speak no more. Many great people have made a substantial difference in our history and left an enduring mark in human memory. But Jesus Christ is truly *alive* now—not only in our remembrance, but in the really real, active and available to all those who open their hearts to him. He dwarfs all the traditional religious categories such as priest, shaman, sacred writer, oracle, preacher, prophet, and so on. Jesus Christ is altogether incomparable, and he remains the same "yesterday, and today, and forever" (Heb. 13:8).

Christ surpasses the ancient sages who have left us their insightful aphorisms; he is the very Word who enlightens all who believe in him. Christ exceeds the learned philosophers who have handed down their reflections to us; he is the Way, the Truth, and the Life for all who hope in him. Christ transcends the mystic visionaries who have shared with us their experience of encountering the holy interiorly; he is the Son-of-God-in-power who pours forth his Holy Spirit upon all who open their hearts to him.

We focus then upon a divine person who is ineffable mystery as God-made-human. Jesus is the perfect image of the Father's knowledge. He is God's subsistent Word, God's absolute wisdom, and God's reflective splendor. It is this same Son, who possesses the one divine nature in common with his Father and his Holy Spirit, who has become one of us human beings forever. We understand all things human as we fix our eyes upon him.

Christ, Our Horizon

Christ is also the horizon of our vision. Jesus is, indeed, divine, but he is also our compassionate elder brother, and we can relate to him as brothers/sisters in friendship—on a human level and in human terms. Jesus is the eternal Son of God, but he is also the Son of Mary, and we can pursue our human pilgrimage in his company. Jesus is divine perfection, but he is also the model of human virtues, and we can imitate him by word and gesture. Jesus is God the Son, but he is also our head and bridegroom, and we can unite with him jointly as one body, one bride.

We should realize that our Lord's humanity is especially significant *for us*. As we recite in the Nicene Creed, God the Son became incarnate "for us men (human beings) and for our salvation." We rejoice not so much in Christ's divinity as in his transfigured humanity. We lift up our hearts in thanksgiving not because God the Son is divine, but because God the Son became genuinely human within our history, went through actual death into Resurrection, and will finally return in unimaginable glory to consummate his redemptive work.

Through the Incarnation, God the Son has become like us in all things, sin alone excepted. This truth is critically significant for our faith-commitment. As a human being, Jesus lived, suffered, and died among us and for us. In his exaltation, Jesus, the transformed human being, ascended into heaven to become our Savior, our risen Lord, who sends his Holy Spirit upon us. In his enthronement our Jesus has become the human high priest through whom we worship the Father, the human advocate who intercedes for us, and the human mediator who sends the Spirit upon us.

Jesus redeemed us by his Paschal Mystery, that is, by his exodus through the agony of the Cross into the triumph of Easter. Jesus was the New Adam who assumed our alienated condition and broke through all barriers to transforming union with his Father. Jesus denied himself in sacrifice, and the Father embraced him for resurrected life. Jesus emptied himself, and the Father filled him with his Holy Spirit. Jesus had been "Son-of God-in-weakness," but the Father elevated him to become Son-of-God-in-power. Jesus passed over from flesh to spirit, from corruption to incorruption, from mortality to immortality, from ignominious death to glorious life. This Passage, or "Paschal Mystery" of Jesus constitutes our redemption.

Yet there is even more. When Jesus died to himself and commended his spirit to the Father, Jesus validated his own paradoxical insight into the meaning of human life. During Jesus' mortal ministry, he had insisted that self-realization comes only through self-denial; those who humble themselves will be exalted, those who take last place will be first, those who have little will obtain more, and it is better to give than to receive. Just as a grain of wheat must be buried in the earth and die if it is to bear rich fruit, so those who lose their life for Christ's sake will find it. Of course, this teaching is utter foolishness and pathetic weakness by any human standard. Yet this foolishness is Christ, the wisdom of God, and this weakness is Christ, the power of God.

In Catholic spirituality, we acknowledge the lasting significance of being human, the problematic realities of our human condition, the lessons of experience, and the pathway to true happiness. Our spirituality provides answers to our preeminent questions about human existence—our sorrows and our joys, our conflicts and our fulfillments, our life and our death. All those answers contribute to our sense of meaning for our lives, and that central significance is our transforming relationship with Christ.

Christ raises our morality beyond mere rectitude to new life as the Father's children. Christ elevates our good works beyond mere "charity" to service of the kingdom. Christ enlivens our liturgy beyond mere ritual to worship in Spirit and in truth. Christ is our inspiration and our motive, our means and our goal.

Jesus has compassion upon us, and he himself is forgiveness for the sins we daily commit. Jesus dwells within us, and he himself is our life. For our faith is not illusion or even dogmatic conviction, but a personal relationship with Christ. Our hope is not wishful thinking, or even solid trust, but entrance into Christ's Resurrection. Our charity is not pious sentimentality or even fidelity to the "golden rule," but selfless love *(agape)* for others as Christ has first loved us.

Our Catholic Worldview

Our vision also opens out to include the whole world, not only as it is now but also as Christ has destined it to become. Our vision enables us to know how wondrously the story will end. We envision the cosmos in its final transformation where the hungry have been fed, the naked have been clothed, the homeless have been sheltered, and the captives have been set free. We look forward to an alienated world reconciled, a hostile world bound together in friendship, a sick world healed, and a broken world made whole. We know the world that is coming, the New Creation steeped in mercy and transformed by grace, abounding in the Light and bathed in the Holy Spirit. Our vision reaches out to comprise the fullness of the Reign as Jesus has proclaimed it in the Gospel.

By his dialogues, Jesus uncovered the true meaning and purpose of God's *Torah* as preparation for God's Reign. By his sermons, Jesus disclosed the undreamt-of extent of God's love in the Reign. People could dare to call upon their Almighty Creator confidently and even affectionately (as Jesus did) with the intimate title of *Abba* ("Daddy"). After all, the Father cherishes each human being immeasurably more than he cares for the birds of the air or the lilies of the field. People should therefore approach their *Abba* with boundless trust. Those who seek will find, those who ask will receive, and those who knock will have it opened unto them. By his works of healing, Jesus signified that the

Reign was already present and active among us.

Christ in his parables dwelt upon the boundless generosity of his Father's Reign. God by human standards shows no propriety or prudent moderation in his love to overflowing. God, Jesus announced, is like a man who put on a wedding feast for his son and invited all the city's low-class riffraff to enjoy it. (Is that any way to run a wedding feast?) God is like the owner of a vineyard who gave the same and equal pay to all his hired hands, whether they had endured the heat of the whole day or had simply worked for one hour. (Is that any way to maintain good labor relations?)

The Father's Reign, Jesus said, is like a shepherd who leaves ninety-nine safe sheep in order to find one lost sheep. He is happier about the one lost sheep that he finds than he is about the safe ninety-nine. (Is that any way to run a flock?) By the same token, God is like a homemaker who retains nine of ten coins, but scours the house all day until she finds one lost coin. She is more joyful over the found coin than she ever was over the other nine. (Is that any way to run a household?)

Jesus' most wonderful of all parables compares God's Reign of incredible largesse, mercy, and love to that of a certain man who has two sons. One son is dutiful and hardworking while the other son demands his inheritance in advance and leaves for a faraway country, breaking his father's heart. Still, the father will not give up on his wayward son, but daily searches the horizon for some precious glimpse of his son coming home. When the father finally sees his errant son returning, the old man cannot control his joy. He rushes to embrace the boy and insists upon restoring him to every filial privilege, including a ring for his finger, sandals for his feet, and a robe for his back. The father even celebrates his son's recovery with a feast more splendid than anything he had ever done for his other son who had faithfully "kept all the rules." (Is that any way to parent a child?)

Jesus by word and example demonstrated the "foolish" wisdom and the "weak" power of the Father's reign. God loves indiscriminately, making his sun to rise on the bad and the good, his rain to fall upon the unjust and the just. Jesus by his life, death, and Resurrection taught that we must love our enemies, do good to those who hate us, and pray for those who persecute us precisely because our Father loves "foolishly" and "weakly" like that.

Christ has called each of us out of darkness into his own marvelous light. He is the Light of the world, the true Light who enlightens every human being, and he illumines the highest reaches of the cosmos. Christ is the *alpha,* and God has created all things through him. Christ is also the *omega,* and God has ordered all things toward him.

With sharpened awareness of our vision, we have dim but sure access to reality as finally restored in its fullest dimensions. Christ is the Father's Sacrament who betokens all that we are meant to be and are destined to become. He is the Father's symbol through whom we view all humankind in our rebirth as God's children. Through Christ's eyes we perceive a world sinful and wounded, yes, yet redeemed and pregnant with promise. Through his perspective we no longer judge anyone as an enemy but acknowledge every woman as our sister and every man as our brother. Through Christ's magnificent dream we imagine all human beings bonded in love and made whole within an all-inclusive community.

The Christian vision sharpens our perceptions, contextualizes our lives, and structures our attitudes. "He himself is before all things, and in him all things hold together" (Col. 1:17). Of course, we find it difficult to sustain our vision in our secularized world of rugged individualism, asphalt, the Internet, instant gratification, and systemic violence. Through our vision, however, we can break through the veil of material things to the ultimately real wherein Christ is alive and God's Reign is at hand.

In Catholic spirituality we identify with Christ's worldview, and we claim his dream as our own. We embrace Christ's vision of the Reign, and we try to see the redemption of all things through his eyes. We promote the Reign's priority of love, and we uphold the Reign's ideal of loving community. Heaven is our true home, the Communion of Saints is our genuine family.

Thanks to the witness of Dorothy Day and of so many others like her, Catholic spirituality has presently recovered a proper balance between interior, contemplative prayer and exterior, activist involvement in ministry. Thanks to the far-reaching work of Pope John XXIII, Vatican Council II, Pope Paul VI, Pope John Paul II, and Pope Benedict XVI. Catholic spirituality has regained dedication to the service of the world.

In Catholic spirituality, we develop a more evangelical orientation. We respond to Christ's mandate toward social justice and universal peace among humankind. We speak of a preferential option for the "widow and the orphan," the poor, and the disenfranchised. We recognize that the Mass not only enriches our personal lives, but also commissions us to bring Christ and his Gospel to the world.

In Catholic spirituality, we are truly pro-life in the broad terms of the "seamless garment" that promotes the dignity of every human being at every stage of life. We oppose *any* and *all* violence: from verbal abuse to physical assault, from racism and sexism to ageism, from capital punishment to warfare, from economic exploitation to environmental pollution. We protect all that is defenseless and vulnerable, from the unborn to the critically ill, and, yes, our environment, too. We work to bring into being God's Reign of unconditional love throughout the universe.

> *The day will come when, after harnessing space, the winds, the tides and gravitation, we shall harness for God the energies of love. And on that day, for the second time in the history of the world, we shall have discovered fire."* (Pierre Teilhard de Chardin)

Toward Reflective Journaling

Faithful discipleship according to Christ's mind and heart requires that we pursue his vision of peace, justice, and love finally to be realized in his kingdom.

QUESTIONS FOR DISCUSSION

1.   How should the Christian disciple's worldview differ from that of the secularist?

2.   To what extent can I look beyond our present world of misery and death to embrace Christ's vision of that glorious future when God will dry every tear from our eyes?

Chapter Three

CHRISTIAN VOICE

*"You are the salt of the earth; but if salt has lost its taste,
how can its saltiness be restored? It is no longer good
for anything, but is thrown out and trampled under
foot. You are the light of the world. A city built on a
hill cannot be hid. No one after lighting a lamp puts it
under the bushel basket, but on the lampstand, and it
gives light to all in the house. In the same way, let your
light shine before others, so that they may see your good
works and glorify your Father in heaven."*
(Matthew 5:13–16)

A PROPHETIC MODEL OF CHRISTIAN VOICE:
THOMAS MERTON, O.C.S.O.

I was still in high school when I first discovered Thomas
Merton. A dear friend told me of Merton's best-selling
autobiography, *The Seven Storey Mountain*, and his adventure
with God intrigued me. As I became more acquainted with
this Trappist monk, I joined the many others who found
inspiration in his description of contemplative prayer.

I was particularly thankful that God had raised up
this prophetic figure within the Church. In the years after

World War II, many American Catholics were reaching a new maturity in their faith, and they were hungering for deeper prayer-life and spirituality. Thomas Merton produced one book after another with clarity and infectious enthusiasm. He had attained spiritual wisdom, and he could communicate it superbly well.

Beyond all question, Thomas Merton (or to use his monastic name, Father Louis, O.C.S.O.) made an incalculable impact upon Catholic consciousness during the twentieth century. He won the esteem of laity, clergy, and Religious alike. When we read one of Merton's books, we communed with him as a fellow disciple and even as a friend. We came to know and even love the man, since he revealed so much of himself in his writings. My generation was particularly proud of Thomas Merton, and we would have been excited to meet him in person.

Adult convert and monk, poet and mystic, essayist and social critic, Thomas Merton became our premier authority on Catholic spirituality. He interpreted the monastic vocation and its significance for the universal Church. Many young people themselves felt an attraction to monastic life when they learned of Merton's experience. Cloistered though he was, Merton carried on a voluminous correspondence with his many friends, and he engaged wholeheartedly in interreligious dialogue with Buddhist monks.

Thomas Merton was a flesh-and-blood saint for our time. He served at Gethsemani Abbey as novice master for a while, yet he never ceased to struggle with his own weaknesses and temptations. Merton possessed uncommon talent as a writer, yet he produced his many books only by disciplined labor. He lived apart from the world, yet he embraced people everywhere with a universal compassion.

Merton's voice reminded us of other great mystics in our tradition. When he recounted his spiritual journey to Catholicism, we thought of another autobiographer, St. Augustine of Hippo. When Merton reached out to the greater Church from his monastic solitude, we recalled another Cistercian monk, St. Bernard of Clairvaux. When Merton insisted upon the real demands of the Gospel in terms of peacemaking, we remembered another radical of Christ, St. Francis of Assisi.

Thomas Merton never ceased to grow in wisdom from his conversion to Catholicism until his untimely death at the age of fifty-three. He remained a committed disciple of Jesus Christ, yet he could claim the powerful truth of nonviolence from a Hindu, Mahatma Gandhi. Merton sustained his deep roots within the Catholic tradition, yet he was able to appropriate some insights of Zen into his approach to meditation. Merton lived and prayed as a Trappist monk, yet he recognized his brother in Thich Nhat Han, a Buddhist monk who protested against the tragic war in Vietnam. Merton received his abbot's special permission to adopt a hermit's solitude, yet he cried out on behalf of the oppressed, the poor, and the needy everywhere.

Even though Merton lived in physical separation from others, he felt an embracing love for all human-kind. Merton's monastic vocation had removed him from the world, but it could not possibly separate him from it. Father Louis, the monk of silence and mystical contemplation, proclaimed his indissoluble unity with all his sisters and brothers.

Thomas Merton insisted upon the priority of human persons over things such as money, technology, and property. Merton voiced his support for the African-American movement for civil rights, and he spoke out for peace in Vietnam. He sensitized our social conscience by exposing the seductive evils of our day for their utter vanity and emptiness. He critiqued our consumerism, our materialism, and our self-indulgence as cruel illusions that could not possibly deliver the fulfillment that they promised.

Thomas Merton protested against all the assaults on human dignity that divided people against one another. He realized, of course, that some kinds of violence were blatant and obviously lethal, such as riot police attacking peaceful demonstrators in the American South and our government prosecuting an unjust war in Vietnam. He also recognized that the systemic violence of racial discrimination and dehumanizing materialism was no less deadly.

It is paradoxical that Thomas Merton should have been such a powerful prophet of Christian voice. As a Trappist, he committed himself to a lifetime of extraordinary silence, yet he raised his voice to enlighten the minds of millions. As a monk, he lived within a strictly cloistered enclosure, yet he projected his voice beyond monastery walls to resound within the hearts of Catholics and non-Catholics everywhere. He summoned us all to live out the Gospel of Christ. He encouraged us to develop deeper prayer-life and spirituality. He persuaded us to share his passion for peace and social justice. Thomas Merton's books remain popular today, and his Christian voice will long continue to resonate among us.

The Theme of Christian Voice

Christian *voice* is our sharing in the voice of Christ. We respond to Christ's vocation and we follow him as disciples in the holy Church; we must, therefore, sound forth our faith-commitment. We must confess our Christian identity, and we must articulate the Christian meaning of our life. We must somehow communicate with God and with one another in terms of our vision and our values.

We cannot sustain any significant relationship without interpersonal dialogue. Many of us have seen a dear friendship atrophy— not because of a quarrel or even because of a misunderstanding, but merely because we stopped communicating and "drifted away." Our discipleship to Christ unites us through him with the Father, and so we must converse with our God in prayer. Our discipleship in the holy Church binds us communally with one another, and so we must dialogue with many people according to multiple levels of relationship.

Christian voice is the forceful expression of our deepest Catholic identity. It is a precious privilege, but it is also a sacred obligation. No matter how blessed or limited we may be in terms of rhetorical skill, all of us must be women and men of prayer and mission. No matter how advanced or rudimentary our training may be, all of us must be people of worship and service. No matter how eloquent or inarticulate we may be, all of us must join in the joyful proclamation that Jesus Christ is Lord.

Two factors provide the background for our Christian voice. First, the Holy Spirit has bound each of us to Christ. This special relationship is peculiarly our own. It is singularly one-on-one; it has never existed before, and it will never be repeated. Therefore, each of us has been commissioned to a unique utterance. Second, each of us develops our personal relationship with Christ through and within the holy Church. Consequently, each of us must participate in the communal voice of our brothers and sisters in Christ.

In Catholic spirituality, our Christian voice always derives its content from Jesus Christ and his Gospel, but it takes form in terms of particularized cultural emphases and from a concrete historical perspective. We may communicate our thoughts and feelings by vocal word, of course, but also by loving gesture and selfless service. We may symbolize our vision not only by art and architecture, but also by music, poetry, and dance.

In this chapter we shall examine three privileged instances of Christian voice: (1) our personal prayer, (2) our liturgical celebration, and (3) our apostolic witness.

Our Personal Prayer

When we pray, we raise our minds and hearts to God. This we must do always, humbly and persistently, even as our lungs must breathe and our hearts must beat. If we truly believe, we absolutely *need* to voice our relationship with the God of truth, beauty, and love. We must open ourselves to the divine renewal and refreshment that remain always available to us. We must cry out from our radical loneliness to commune with the divine presence. We must reach outward from our deep-seated thirst to drink from the divine wisdom. We must stretch forth from our foundational hunger to bask in the divine communion.

By Christ's redemptive grace, we have been empowered to relate to each of the divine persons. Occasionally we may pray directly to the Holy Spirit, who purifies, guides, and sanctifies us. Very often we may pray directly to Christ, who is our mediator, high priest, and best of all friends. But when we pray *to* God the Father *through* Jesus Christ *in* the Holy Spirit, we voice our wondrous dignity as God's adoptive children and express the very rhythm of our salvation.

Of course, we may freely choose to pray from a wide

variety of forms. We may pray individually in the privacy of our bedroom, or we may pray communally in the liturgy of our parish church. We may pray vocally, whether by spontaneous utterance or by traditional formula. We may recite a single prayer with concentrated thoughtfulness, or we may pray repetitively as we do in the Rosary or in a traditional litany. We may pray serenely and peacefully as we give thanks to God, or we may even speak out boldly as we struggle with God. We may pray in adoration, in contrition, or in supplication. In all of these ways, we surely pray in the Spirit and in truth so long as we truly turn toward the God who constantly fixes his divine gaze upon us.

We are also free to choose from a variety of methods in our prayer. We may pray mentally by centered reflection and by spiritual reading. We may progress in the art of praying from traditional formulas to discursive meditation, and even, perhaps, from affective aspirations to simple contemplation. We may also pray with our hands through almsgiving and service to others, with our stomachs by fasting, and with our feet by pilgrimage. We may even make a prayer of our work and our recreation, so long as we plunge into life wholeheartedly for the praise of the glory of God's grace.

Our every thought, aspiration, and deed can be genuine prayer so long as we are raising our mind and heart to God in the midst of it; even our calm silence before God can voice our willing receptivity to God's dynamic presence. Often it suffices simply to be quiet: "Be still, and know that I am God!" (Psalms 46:10). A man who used to sit for hours in St. Jean Vianney's parish of Ars explained simply to his pastor, "I look at God and God looks at me."

We may voice our discipleship through sacred hymnody. As St. Augustine observed, "The one who sings prays twice." We may even pray with wordless music. Music becomes the language of the soul when prosaic words are inadequate for the task. A German plaque reads: "Bach gave us God's Word; Mozart gave us God's laughter; Beethoven gave us God's fire; God gave us music that we might pray without words."

Whatever the form, our prayer must open to personal presence—vulnerable availability to God. We have all had the disappointing experience of conversing with someone for several minutes only to realize that our friend who stares at us is actually "a million miles away." Physical proximity facilitates personal presence, but it may also disguise a spiritual absence. In merely physical presence, we draw close to someone in a quantitative way. In personal presence, however, we become accessible to another person in knowledge, freedom, and love. In prayer, we become present to God in mind and heart under the impulse of divine grace.

First, we become available in heightened awareness to the God who is always present in knowing us. We raise our minds to know God with intellectual *attention*. In order to do this effectively, we need to collect our thoughts and sharpen our focus upon God despite the inevitable distractions that may occupy us. As King Claudius observes in Shakespeare's *Hamlet*, "My words fly up, my thoughts remain below; words without thoughts never to heaven go."

Second, we lift up ourselves in self-donation to the God who is always present in loving us. We raise our hearts to cling to God with volitional intention. In order to achieve this adherence, we must discipline our affections and deliver ourselves to God despite the many attachments that may restrain us. That is why the celebrant of the Mass always invites the congregation to join in the Eucharistic Prayer with the summons: "Lift up your hearts!"

Finally, our prayerful voice is altogether a matter of divine grace. We need to invoke the Holy Spirit's assistance. The Spirit can hone our minds out of their dullness; the Spirit can moisten our hearts out of their dryness. The Holy Spirit prays for us and in us "with unspeakable groanings," when we know not what to say.

It is encouraging to realize that we need not compete with billions of other human beings for God's attention and intention, since our God is boundlessly self-giving. God can welcome each of us as though we were God's only creature. We need not summon God to us, since our God is already available to us here and now, everywhere and always.

The necessary precondition for effective prayer is our absolute conviction that God loves us and embraces us with mercy. Indeed, God is actively present to us, and God's love for us is uniquely personalized and compassionate. In theory, it is a simple matter to raise our minds and our hearts to our wonderful God, but in practice prayer can be an arduous challenge.

By prayer, we disclose ourselves in unreserved openness before our God of love. But remorse for failings of the past, anxiety over challenges of the present, and fear about unknown vicissitudes of the future may obstruct our turning. By prayer, we dispose ourselves in naked vulnerability before our God of compassion, but disorderly self-love may undermine our confidence. We shall never pray well if we entertain the slightest doubt about God's enduring concern for us. We journey forward, protected by God's providence, guided by God's wisdom, and steeped in God's mercy.

Prayer is a *healing* experience. We become whole as we present ourselves before our God of purifying mercy. We gain confidence as we awaken to God's restorative love. When we believe with our whole minds and hope with our whole hearts, we can move on beyond painful memories of the past, confront future difficulties, and embrace life fully in the present.

Prayer is an *elevating* experience. It enlightens us as we realize our conditioned creaturehood, our contingency, and our radical dependency upon God. It raises our awareness of our God. It deepens our consciousness of our basic unity within humankind, since all women and men of every ethnicity and religious tradition are our sisters and brothers in God's human family.

Prayer is a *transforming* experience. When we pray, the Spirit deepens our daughtership/sonship in Christ so that we cry out "*Abba,* dear Father!" We approach the Father on our own behalf and in behalf of others. We open our minds and hearts to the Father who loves us faithfully and compassionately. We raise our minds and hearts to the Father with prayers of adoration, of supplication, of repentance, and, most especially, of gratitude.

When we *remember*, we recall our radical poverty and our indebtedness to the Father for all God's gifts that nourish and sustain our lives. Prayerful remembrance orients our lives, humbles our souls, and restores our grasp on reality. Prayerful remembrance deepens our sense of absolute contingency in the loving embrace of our Father. To forget is to become an ingrate, and forgetfulness is an occupational hazard of our human condition. Yet prayerful remembrance makes us acknowledge all the blessings for which we must break into joyful thanksgiving.

If we are to strengthen our personal relationship with our God, we must sustain regular communication. We need daily to converse with God in an ongoing dialogue of speaking and listening. We are God's holy people, and each of us individually is graced to be God's holy woman or God's holy man. God's holy woman has to be a woman who prays, and God's holy man has to be a man who prays.

There can be no substitute for our prayer, and there can be no dispensation from our obligation to pray.

We do not pray in order to change the will of God; we pray rather in order to conform ourselves to God's will. As Jesus prayed in Gethsemani, "Father, if you are willing, remove this cup from me; yet, not my will but yours be done'" (Luke 22:42). We submit our minds to the saving truths of God's revelation. We offer our hearts in unreserved forgiveness, acceptance, and reconciliation with one another.

Our Liturgical Celebration

The psalmist urges us, "Make a joyful noise to God, all the earth; Sing the glory of his name; give to him glorious praise" (Psalms 66:1–2). Our Mass is the great Christian prayer of gratitude. Gathered in community, we cry out through Christ, our mediator and high priest. When we participate deliberately in the eucharistic liturgy, our Christian voice finds congregational expression. Our communal acclamations reach through Christ to the very throne of our Heavenly Father.

Our celebration of the Holy Eucharist on the Lord's Day has to be the high point of our week. Our brief time at Mass is "our finest hour," when we discover our most authentic selves. We are still the Church from moment to moment, of course, even when we are dispersed in all directions and appear to be separated individuals. When we gather together for Mass, however, we show forth all that we actually are as a sacred community, with one Lord, one faith, one hope, and one love. We actualize symbolically our truest identity as disciples of Christ in his holy Church.

With ecclesial voice, we co-offer the Holy Eucharist as the sacramental fountain of our Christian life. All that we attempt to do in Christ draws its power from the altar, whether it be our interior growth, our organized parochial ministries, or our personal connections with the greater community. Our Mass is also the sacramental pinnacle of our Christian life. All that we actually achieve in Christ receives its climactic crowning at the sacred table, whether it be catechumenal formation, catechetical instruction, celebration of the other six sacraments, or service of the poor and needy

With Christian voice, we jointly encounter our Risen Lord in Word and Sacrament. "It is the Mass that matters," because the Holy Eucharist effectively signifies everything that God is and will be for us, from the Creation of the world to the Second Coming of Christ. The Mass is our ritual memorial and representation of Christ's Paschal Mystery for our salvation. The Mass is our sacrifice of praise and thanksgiving to God. The Mass is even the forgiveness of the sins we daily commit. Our eucharistic celebration is the pledge of our enduring life and the seed of our final resurrection within the Communion of Saints.

With communal voice, we worship the Father through Christ in the Holy Spirit, and we pray in the first person plural. Together we sing our hymns, together we confess the Nicene Creed, and together we affirm the Eucharistic Prayer with our Great Amen. We exchange the kiss of peace and reconciliation with one another in familial affection. "The cup of blessing that we bless, is it not a sharing in the blood of Christ? The bread that we break, is it not a sharing in the body of Christ? Because there is one bread, we who are many are one body, for we all partake of the one bread" (1 Corinthians 10:16–17).

Our Apostolic Witness

Our Christian voice also finds expression through the witness of our lives. We demonstrate our faith-commitment to Christ not only by the words of our mouths, but also by the creativity of our minds, the affection of our hearts, and the symbolic gestures of our bodies. Indeed, we find here a pointed validation of the old adage: "Actions speak louder than words."

We utter a compassionate voice when we serve our fellow human beings. Our Holy Tradition has identified seven preeminent works that can demonstrate Christian love and social justice. These "corporal works of mercy" are: (1) feed the hungry, (2) give drink to the thirsty, (3) welcome the stranger; (4) clothe the naked, (5) visit the sick, (6) visit the prisoner, and (7) bury the dead. There are always more needs for service than we can possibly meet, but we must respond with generosity and spontaneity.

We speak with a supportive voice when we use our gifts and talents to be Christ for others. Catholic tradition lists seven critical services that can share Christian wisdom and understanding. These "spiritual works of mercy" are: (1) convert the sinner, (2) instruct the ignorant, (3) counsel the doubtful, (4) comfort the sorrowful, (5) bear wrongs patiently, (6) forgive injuries, and (7) pray for the living and the dead. If we truly want to be there for others, we shall always discover more opportunities for giving.

We speak a persuasive voice when we join in the Church's mission of evangelization to individuals, to our community, and even to the world at large. If we are truly disciples of Christ, it follows that we are disciples of Christ *in mission*. By virtue of our baptism and confirmation, we have been sent to proclaim Christ to all who do not know him. We must bear witness about Christ to others, and nobody can dispense us from this privilege and obligation.

> *But just as we have the same spirit of faith that is in accordance with scripture—"believed, and so I spoke"— we also believe, and so we speak....* (2 Cor. 4:13).

Toward Reflective Journaling

Faithful discipleship according to Christ's mind and heart requires that we express our love for others by generous service and communicate our love for God by "praying always."

QUESTIONS FOR DISCUSSION

1.   By what various ways can I give voice to my personal faith in Christ?

2.   How can I with my special gifts join my voice to the communal voice of Christ's holy Church?

Chapter Four

CHRISTIAN VALUES

Finally, beloved, whatever is true, whatever is honorable, whatever is just, whatever is pure, whatever is pleasing, whatever is commendable, if there is any excellence and if there is anything worthy of praise, think about these things. (Philippians 4:8)

A PROPHETIC MODEL OF CHRISTIAN VALUES: JACQUES MARITAIN, PH.D.

I have not enjoyed the privilege of actually meeting my favorite philosopher, although I struggled mightily to understand his books on Catholic thought. I cannot even say that I followed his personal history from afar, although I occasionally joined in spirited discussion of his many virtues. So far as I was concerned, he was a venerable but distant teacher-scholar ensconced at Princeton University. Nevertheless, I did revere the great professor Jacques Maritain: a contemporary Catholic who combined towering intellect with mystical holiness.

While Maritain was still a nonbeliever, he found a soul mate in the Jewess Raissa Ousmanoff, and they confirmed their spiritual bond in marriage. Raissa, in her book *We Have*

Been Friends Together, describes the personalist relationships they enjoyed together as a couple. One friend, Leon
Bloy, introduced them to the study of St. Thomas Aquinas's
Summa Theologica, and they learned to appreciate the enduring values of the Catholic tradition. After an intensive quest
together, Raissa and Jacques embraced the Catholic faith
and centered the communion with God for which they had
so deeply hungered. Upon Raissa's death, Jacques joined the
Little Brothers of Jesus at Toulouse, France. Later still, he
became a cardinal of the Roman Church.

Jacques Maritain was a philosopher of masterful ratio-
nality, but he also possessed the intuitive power of the artist and the poet. He authored some fifty books—not only
on metaphysics, but also on ethics, aesthetics, and human
personhood. He confessed that he truly loved St. Thomas
and the philosophical theology that bears his name, yet he
was also an advanced contemplative of mystical faith. He
vigorously championed the cause of Christian humanism
on two continents and bequeathed a spiritual legacy for
generations to come.

Jacques Maritain was able by exhaustive study, reflection,
and prayer in the Holy Spirit to wed a rigorous intellectual
life with uncommon sanctity. This gentle, retiring, white-
haired gentleman of academe will always hold a secure place
in my personal gallery of heroes. Maritain was a prophetic
model, because he bore witness in the public arena to the
principal values of Catholic spirituality. He once wrote: "It

shall revive, a new civilization shall come to life on condition that it hope for, and will, and love truly and heroically, truth, beauty, and fraternity." Amen, indeed.

The Theme of Christian Values

As disciples of Christ in his holy Church, we must live by the same *values* that informed the wisdom of our master. Christ's realization of the substantively true as distinguished from vain illusions must inspire our understanding. Christ's embrace of the objectively good as contrasted with self-interested projects must guide our prudential judgments. Christ's thanksgiving for the enduringly beautiful as opposed to superficial attractions must motivate our pursuits.

Our "values" include all that we hold as primarily important in our lives. They are our guiding lights, no matter the darkness that may envelop us; they remain our oases of renewal, no matter the wilderness that may surround us. Accordingly we "value" our spiritual ideals, we cherish our most meaningful aspirations, and we nurture our noblest, most admirable human qualities. So it is that we prize our nonnegotiable standards of morality as our conscientious criteria for virtuous activity. Thus we esteem our principles of practical wisdom as we sort out our priorities and determine our life's agenda.

As Christian disciples in mission, we must gradually appropriate the values of our Savior so that we may live by them ourselves and promote them in the lives of others. We have to place Christ's values into first place within our minds and into front and center place within our hearts. We must learn to appreciate as Our Lord does all that is lastingly true, unexceptionally good, and enduringly beautiful. In this way we may participate in the very spirituality of Jesus.

We cannot compromise, manipulate, or exploit our Christian values. Unless we sustain our values intact, our spirituality can become empty—much ado about nothing. By reflective prayer and faithful devotion to Our Lord throughout our journey, however, Christ's priorities, concerns, and preferential options can gradually become instinctive constituents of our own personal character.

In this chapter we shall consider some principal values of Christian discipleship: (1) our natural goodness as creatures of God, (2) our human personhood and our personal relationships, and (3) our community and our holy Tradition in Christ.

Our Natural Goodness as Creatures of God

Our Lord knew that his Father had created the whole universe and declared all of it to be not only good but "very good" (Gen. 1:31). God's initial blessing endures, of course, as a lasting approval and endorsement, despite any subsequent sinfulness on the part of human beings.

Consequently, Christ rejoiced in the goodness of the material world and of all God's creatures within it. Our Lord exulted in their very being, and he praised his Father for their beauty. Above all, Christ acknowledged the inherent goodness of human beings in themselves and as such, despite any of their moral lapses and even before their final transformation.

We who follow Christ as his disciples must esteem all creatures as he does. It is a classical principle of Catholic wisdom that grace always builds on nature (and does not displace it). Accordingly, we do not see our humanity as irremediably corrupted by sin in its very essence.

Even though our humanity has been wounded by sinfulness, it has retained its basic potential for divine restoration and elevation. The grace of the Holy Spirit perfects (and does not substitute for) our human life. God's grace does not merely cover over our transgressions; it actually removes our sins and purifies us from their consequences. God's grace does not simply clothe over our failings so that they are not imputed to us; it genuinely sanctifies us interiorly after the likeness of the Risen Christ.

By the same token, Catholicism affirms (and does not denigrate) the natural moral law that is written in the human heart, even as it proclaims Christ's commandment of love that enlivens our faith. Catholicism insists upon the goodness of this material world, even as it confesses faith in its ultimate renovation when Christ returns.

Catholic spirituality acknowledges our material body in this life, even as it confesses faith in our final resurrection in the world to come.

In our Catholic worldview, faith perfects natural reason. Our intellect has become clouded by sin, yet it can still know what is true. Therefore, the grace of faith illumines (and does not contradict) our power of understanding. From the same perspective, Christian liberty perfects our natural freedom. Our will has indeed become weakened by sin, yet it can still love what is good. The Holy Spirit works gently and concordantly within our freedom in order to lead us to our fulfillment in the holy liberty of God's children. God's grace of charity heals and elevates (but does not constrain) our capacity for selfless service to others.

After all, we appreciate many nonliving things as significant for our well-being, such as the resources of the earth, a pleasant environment, an efficient workplace, warm clothing, nourishing food, and an inviting home. God provides us with such inanimate things for the enhancement of our lives, and we human beings are permitted to utilize them as a means toward our own fullness of life.

We also esteem many living things as worthy adjuncts to our fulfillment, such as the plants, the animals, the fish, and the birds that share our world. We feel bound to reverence all living things precisely because they are alive. Yet we remain free to use them for the sake of our own more complete life.

Our Human Personhood and Our Personal Relationships

In our Catholic spirituality, we value our human personhood and our personal relationships. We esteem all people, because our God has created us after God's own image and likeness. Indeed, God cherishes us human persons as God's foremost creatures in the whole universe: "Look at the birds of the air; they neither sow nor reap nor gather into barns, and yet your heavenly Father feeds them. Are you not of more value than they?" (Matt. 6:26). Thus Our Lord has revealed the Father's wondrous love for all of us.

Our heavenly Father has gifted each of us with the inherent dignity of personhood, and no one has the right to dehumanize us. Each one of us can say that our birth was a spectacular event for the world. Each one of us appeared here by no random accident, but only by God's specific purpose and divine intervention. Each one of us can confess in all humility, "God has never created anybody quite like me before, and there will never be anyone quite like me again."

God has rooted inviolable human rights within our personhood. We are autonomous within ourselves and not slaves; no one else has the right to own us. In our personhood we are ends in ourselves and not manipulable tools; no one else has the right to make us the means to a further purpose. We are the subjects of inalienable rights; no one else has the right to exploit us.

For example, God has endowed our personhood with the right to life, the right to marry, and the right to our good name. God has also granted us the right freely to follow our conscience, the right to earn a saving, family wage in exchange for our labor, and the right to property. God has even emblazoned our personhood with immortality, and each of us will live into God's eternity.

God has created us as a marvelous composite of material body and spiritual soul, both of which are good in their entirety and both of which are extremely essential to our complete humanity. Our personhood, however, finds its roots within our spiritual soul with its inherent powers of intellect and free will; it is in our human spirit that we find our very capacity for a spiritual life and for spirituality. Moreover, it is because we are spiritual persons that God can transform us through Christ in the Holy Spirit, causing us to begin, develop, and mature in our Catholic spirituality.

A major consequence of our personhood is our capacity for entering enriching personal relationships. God has given us as persons the wondrous capacity to bond mutually and spiritually with one another. The Father has crafted the power of relationality into our personhood, so that we can connect spiritually with other human persons by knowledge and by love in freedom. Because God has made us as embodied spirits, we can transcend the physical limitations that separate us from other persons.

In our Catholic spirituality, therefore, we also place primary value upon our personal relationships that fill life with meaning; merely material things, however desirable, must of necessity take second place. Our personal relationships include all those special bonds among people that gratify our hearts and make our lives worth living. Our most precious relationships unite husband to wife in our marriages, parents to children in our families, and heart to heart in our friendships.

In our finest moments, we esteem our personal relationships beyond all price and before any merely physical good. What does it mean for us if we achieve major financial success but at the cost of a broken marriage? Where is the percentage in winning social fame if we lose our children's affection in the process? Can anyone who has consistently failed to bond with others ever be rated as a successful human being? Among life's most painful tragedies is not economic deprivation, but a personal relationship reduced to bankruptcy.

Our personal relationships demand self-transcendence and mutual fidelity, but they prosper most of all when we gradually learn to love beyond self-interest as God loves. Indeed, our experience of personal relationships distantly reflects the inner life of God, wherein the Father, the Son, and the Holy Spirit abide as subsistent relationships of lover, loved, and love.

Christ's Gospel assures us that in our personhood we can even transcend the immeasurable chasm of infinity that separates us from God. Of course, we cannot possibly reach out to God, but God has already reached out to us.

By God's grace we can enter a personal relationship with the Father through Christ in the Holy Spirit. As wayfarers in this present life, we can relate to God by the Spirit's unifying gifts of faith, hope, and charity. As glorified saints in the world to come, we can relate to God by the Spirit's unifying gift of the beatific vision.

Our Community and Our Holy Tradition in Christ

Bonded community has been a salient feature of Catholic spirituality from the very beginning. Of course, even as human beings we are spontaneously social, and we naturally long to relate with one another in community. We may want to be freely ourselves, fiercely independent and ruggedly individualistic, yet we can never quite suffocate our hunger for fellowship with others. The poet John Donne recognized our dependence upon one another in his famous lines: "No man is an island, entire of itself; every man is a piece of the continent, a part of the main; if a clod be washed away from sea, Europe is the less as well as if a promontory were." It is not good for us to be alone, and we feel uncomfortable when we must be alone over a long period. We all have a need to belong to some group that reaches out beyond us and shares a further, collective meaning with us.

Catholic spirituality has always placed a premium upon the value of Christian community. For Christ has called us not only to be his personal disciples, but also to enjoy a communion of life within God's holy people. It is by Christ's body and in that body that we belong to Christ. It is in company with the people and through that people that we collaborate on our mission and pursue our pilgrimage to the Father. Consequently, we need to gather with other believers at many levels of reciprocity and mutuality in terms of our particular ministries, our parish life, and, perhaps, our broader diocesan projects.

Our communal bonds vindicate both our theology of Church and our assemblies for sacred liturgy. We most commonly gather together for eucharistic worship, especially on Sunday, the Lord's Day. It is typically Catholic for us to depend upon one another for joint assistance and sustenance in living out our faith-commitment. We pray for one another and we serve one another. We even share our gifts and our shortcomings, our wisdoms and our follies, our stories and our lives. It is not surprising that in recent years, Catholics in large parishes have spontaneously joined together as friends in what are called "small communities."

We vigorously affirm the Christian family, wherein a woman and a man create their own community of love in Christ for the interchange of mutual love and for the nurture of children. It is in family life that most of us learn to make our initial steps back to the Father. Ordinarily we must first enjoy our parents' selfless love given to us for our own sakes, and this experience primes us for loving others. Within our families, we can readily share our feelings and our thoughts, our losses and our triumphs, our aspirations and our prayers. We nourish our own self-esteem as irreplaceable members of the familial community, and we give of ourselves for the sake of the whole.

Catholicism has fostered the monastic communities of nuns and monks who devote themselves to a life of contemplative prayer and self-denial. Religious orders and congregations of sisters, brothers, and clerics have multiplied over the centuries. We have developed the third orders secular that allow laypeople to pursue a lay lifestyle but still join together regularly for spiritual renewal and growth. We especially value our greater community in the body of Christ, the holy Church.

So it has been from our earliest days as Church: "They devoted themselves to the apostles' teaching and fellowship, to the breaking of bread and the prayers" (Acts 2:42). Together and not singly, we are "the called" *(Ekklesia)*. Together and not singly, we have become God's people of the new covenant. Together and not singly (however inadequately), we must symbolize the mystery of Christ's redeeming presence in the world.

It is distinctively Catholic for us to root our spirituality within that living heritage known as "Tradition." Catholic Tradition is our joint experience of the Risen Christ among us in the Spirit over the centuries—the cumulative response of billions of believers. Catholic Tradition is a legacy in depth—not only humanly fallible but also divinely infallible, not only institutionally structured but also spiritually personalist, not only dogmatically defined but also dynamically developing. We revere this great Tradition that is not only one, holy, and apostolic, but also enduringly Catholic.

We have been called to possess our spiritual inheritance for the totality of life. Our Tradition encompasses all the riches for which the gathered people of God is both repository and channel. Millions of our forebears have drawn upon this sacred legacy even as millions more have contributed to its further deepening. Tradition gives us our worldview, but it also guides us in interpreting its contents. Tradition nourishes us for living out our spirituality: our conceptual categories for theologizing, our proper language for sharing and praying, and our motivation for growing in love. We especially value this great Tradition; for it constitutes our religious identity—what our Church has gratefully received from our foremothers and forefathers, but also handed forward.

Our Tradition contains the sacred liturgy. In times past, God assembled the people of Israel to offer sacrifice in the desert, and the Jews have remained preeminently a people gathered for worship. God has gathered us, the New Israel, to offer the sacrifice of praise and thanksgiving in Christ, and we shall always be a people of worship. Therefore, the holy Mass is our life's blood. For us, "It is the Mass that matters," and we cannot live without it.

Our Tradition includes our precious sacred scriptures, the Word of God made human words within the Church. Of course, our Tradition is richer than any text, however inspired. We listen to the proclamation of our scriptures especially within our liturgical assembly, and we lovingly embrace their content. We discover foreshadowings of the Risen Christ in the law and the prophets of the Old Testament. We engage ourselves with the Risen Christ who discloses himself in the four Gospels, the epistles, and the other writings of the New Testament. In our Catholic Tradition, we adhere to the biblical principle; because of the Incarnation, we can encounter God through inspired human authors.

Our Tradition also encompasses our defined doctrines, the Revelation of God made verbal formulas within the Church. Of course, our holy Tradition is fuller than any dogmas, however infallible. It looks to extraordinary disciples within the Communion of Saints for exemplifying the holy. It delights in stories that express the true, and it responds to symbolism that embodies the good. It depends upon all the arts for communicating the beautiful: poetry and literature, painting and sculpture, architecture and music. It celebrates the great mysteries of faith in the course of our liturgical year, beginning with Advent.

Our Tradition understands the Church Catholic to be a communion of local churches, as, for example, the church of San Diego, the church of Salzburg, and the church of Milan. A single bishop, assisted by his priests and deacons, mediates the saving presence of Christ our High Priest for each local church or "diocese." Each of us, therefore, connects with the Church Catholic through our sustained communion with our bishop. In the Catholic Tradition, we adhere to the Episcopal Principle; because of the Incarnation, we can encounter God through ordained ministers.

In addition, Tradition includes our particular traditions (with a small "t") such as our style of piety, our sacramentals for various occasions, and our instinctive approach to birth, marriage, and death. We inherit a storehouse of little "traditions," such as the use of the crucifix, scapular medals, shrines, and statues. We also cultivate various practices of devotion such as making the Sign of the Cross, genuflecting before the Blessed Sacrament, and fixing our attention upon the altar with its central crucifix.

Like Tevya in *Fiddler on the Roof*, we value our Tradition, because our Tradition tells us who we are and what God expects us to do. Thus we can interpret the experiences of our life

> *If in the beginning human experience is bitter, with the help of God it can become the source of sweetness.*
> (Raïssa Maritain. Tr. Bernard E. Doering)

Toward Reflective Journaling

Faithful discipleship according to Christ's mind and heart requires that we commit ourselves faithfully to values vastly different from those of our surrounding culture.

QUESTIONS FOR DISCUSSION

1.   How would you articulate your primary values as a disciple of Christ in the holy Church?

2.   In what ways does your faith in the Risen Christ structure your values as you confront the particular challenges in your life?

Chapter Five
CHRISTIAN VOLITION

Therefore, my beloved, just as you have always obeyed me, not only in my presence, but much more now in my absence, work out your own salvation with fear and trembling; for it is God who is at work in you, enabling you both to will and to work for his good pleasure. (Philippians 2:12–13)

A PROPHETIC MODEL OF CHRISTIAN VOLITION: JOAN CHITTESTER, O.S.B.

Sister Joan Chittester, O.S.B., is a strong woman, graced and ennobled by the Holy Spirit. I met her only once, and that briefly, during a reception at St. John's Abbey in Collegeville, Minnesota, but she made a lasting impact on me. I was just beginning a sabbatical semester at the Institute for Ecumenical and Cultural Research, and each of us participants had summarized our research project for the members of the board. As I was returning to my place at the table after my own presentation, Sister Joan, a member of the board, called out to me with her gracious smile and congratulated me on my choice of subject ("Peace and World Religions"). "Good work, George, we need that book!" she exclaimed. Those few words of encouragement meant so much to me.

Christian volition is our *will power*, our determination faithfully to persevere on the path Christ has laid out for us. It drives our personal self-donation to Christ, and Sister Joan has surrendered herself to our Lord. It bonds us to the Christian community, and Sister Joan has devoted herself to our Church. It motivates our choice of lifestyle within the Church, and Sister Joan has vowed herself to Our Lord according to the Rule of St. Benedict.

Volition fires up our love for God and energizes our love for our fellow human beings; Sister Joan has determined to be a loving woman. Volition fortifies our conscientious decisions in the face of opposition; Sister Joan has proved resolute despite the negative criticisms that prophets must always endure. Christian volition requires communal support; Sister Joan Chittester has depended upon her Benedictine Order for discriminating counsel and hopeful encouragement.

Sister Joan Chittester is an enthusiastic disciple of Jesus Christ. She not only sustains her deep roots within her order, but also interprets Benedictine spirituality for the Church at large. Sister Joan is a world-class speaker, who fearlessly and willingly proclaims the Gospel in the public arena. She works ardently to vindicate women's rightful role in the Church and in society, but she also advocates human rights, peace, and justice for everyone. Sister Joan maintains her inner fortress of faith, peace, and joy despite the harsh barbs of the unfair who contest her presence and her message.

Sister Joan Chittester partners with others in theological dialogue, conducts retreats, and delivers keynote addresses nationally and internationally. She directs Benetvision: A Resource and Research Center for Contemporary Spirituality. Sister Joan has been prioress of the Benedictine Sisters of Erie and president both of the Conference of American Benedictine Prioresses and of the Leadership Conference of Women Religious. She is also a weekly columnist for the *National Catholic Reporter* and an author of twenty-two successful books. Sister Joan Chittester is a courageous prophet who by her graced volition is making a substantive difference for our contemporary Church.

The Theme of Christian Volition

Another essential theme of our Catholic spirituality is Christian *volition*, our participation in the will power of Christ. Here it is imperative that we realize how utterly we depend upon Christ and his Holy Spirit to realize our goals. Christian volition is always a matter of divine grace inspiring our will power. With Christ we can do all things, but without Christ and his grace we can do nothing. As disciples of Christ in mission, we must depend unfailingly upon Christ's Holy Spirit to work within our freedom both to will and to accomplish.

Jesus prayed that his Father's will, not his own, be done. Mary freely consented to the Angel Gabriel's invitation to become mother of the Savior. All our saints through history have been persons of uncommon volition. St. Paul the Apostle, for example, endured crushing afflictions during his apostolate, but he determinedly stood his ground: "I have fought the good fight, I have finished the race, I have kept the faith" (2 Tim. 4:7). He attributed his strength of will to God's grace, active within him through his very weakness.

The Father has endowed our personhood with the faculty of free will. By our *intellectual attention*, we know Christ and his Church, and we understand the implications of our Christian discipleship. We can master information about the historical Jesus, and we can also come to know the living Christ in personal relationship. We can study the works of our great "doctors," and we can also retrieve the vast riches of our Catholic Tradition. We can reflect intellectually upon theology, and we can also savor the wisdom that flows from love (*sapientia*, Latin for "wisdom," literally means "tasting knowledge").

We must call upon our *volitional intention*, however, if we are freely to decide for Christ and to assent to our Christian vocation. Further, we must also determine subsequent choices that necessarily flow from our basic decision. By our volition, we submit ourselves to Christ's discipline and we become Christian disciples. Consequently, we deliver our minds and hearts to Christ to become Christ-motivated, we surrender our activities to Christ to become Christ-oriented, and we hand over our lives to Christ to become Christ-directed.

By our volition, we discipline our blind instincts and we order our unruly passions. We direct our moral actions and we lead a life of integrity. We confront critical challenges and we make crucial decisions. We consider multiple options and we make accountable choices. We relate to some persons with friendship and to all other persons with civility and respect.

Without volition, we shall contribute little or nothing toward Christ's kingdom. Without heartfelt resolve, we shall allow our good intentions to remain no more than mere velleities, such as "I wish...," "Wouldn't it be nice if someday..." or "I have been thinking that I really should..." Without persevering determination, our vocation becomes an inviting offer, our vision fades into superficial aspiration, and our virtues become ineffectual inclinations. Without decisive execution, we may talk a good path, but we shall not walk it. Devoid of volition, we become weak and idle spectators, we bear no fruit, and we make no difference.

On the first Christmas morning, the angelic hosts proclaimed peace to people of goodwill. It is therefore a matter of our graced resolve to become *good* persons, faithful disciples, loving people. We must actuate our gifts, serve others, and carry our plans forward. We need by graced freedom to control our lives, pursue our goals, and create our future under God.

In this chapter we shall consider volition from the following three perspectives: (1) our engagement with Christ, (2) our commitment to the Church, and (3) our life of Faith.

Our Engagement with Christ

Every element of our Catholic faith converges upon Jesus Christ. As we grow to adulthood, we become aware of the many religious options available to us. We learn that there have been other teachers of wisdom who have left behind living traditions, and millions of people find their teachings uplifting. Nevertheless, we ourselves, aware of our alternatives and in full command of our freedom, joyfully commit ourselves to the Risen Christ.

By our faith we reach a heightened consciousness that breaks beyond our visible world and rests upon the Risen Lord in whom all things hold together. We attain a sharpened awareness that penetrates our shadowy horizons and distinguishes the transfigured Christ in whose light we see light. We enjoy an enlightened perspective that fastens upon Christ, the one still-Point who gives all things their meaning.

Our faith is a happy knowledge that perfects our reason and enlightens our intellect: "And this is eternal life, that they may know you, the only true God, and Jesus Christ whom you have sent" (John 17:3). Yet our faith is also a joyful volition that perfects our freedom and energizes our will: "If you continue in my word, you are truly my disciples; and you will know the truth, and the truth will make you free" (John 8:31b–32).

We discover that Christ personifies our every ideal of truth and wisdom, and we want to follow him. We realize that Christ embodies our every value of goodness and holiness, and we long to unite with him. We resonate to the beauty and wonder of the Christian story, and we want to share in it. We determine to surrender to this Jesus who calls us to become his disciples. Therefore, we conclude, it is good and right ("meet and just") for us to believe.

We decide to believe. We wholeheartedly want to believe. Nevertheless, genuine Christian faith results finally from God's gratuitous and unmerited favor. Our vocation to faith is God's gift for each of us personally to nurture and fully to live. Without this grace, we would be powerless to realize our intention.

Catholic theology defines faith as an act of the intellect, moved by the will, under the inspiration of grace to know God's Revelation on the authority of God revealing. (Theologians have a knack for impersonal and abstract analysis.) It seems that five critical elements converge in this single event when we decide to believe.

First, our faith is an act of cognition. In acquiring

Christian truth, our intellect achieves true knowledge. Second, our faith is an act of volition. In the absence of rational evidence, our will freely moves our intellect to assent. Third, our faith depends upon grace. In the attainment of supernal realities beyond us, the Holy Spirit enlightens our intellect and inspires our free will. Fourth, our faith comes to know the Father's self-disclosure. It encounters the Risen Christ, who is very truth. Fifth, our faith rests upon the authority of God revealing. There can be no higher foundation.

God's gift of grace initiates an interpersonal relationship that never stands still. It depends upon regular intercommunication, and its power either increases or declines. With prayer, spiritual exercises, and active participation in worship, we can progress in faith along our way of discipleship. With indifference, we can grow weak in faith, and with neglect, we can even lose our faith all together. Therefore, we need to renew and deepen our faith ever again as we live out our lives. "Lord, Jesus Christ, I believe into you! Help my unbelief!"

This means much more than a cerebral faith that is doctrinally correct and orthodox, yet rarefied, inconsequential, and irrelevant. Christ calls us to give ourselves to him totally and without reserve, with our whole mind, our whole heart, our whole soul, and our whole strength. Christ calls not upon ours but upon ourselves. Christ invites us to enter an abiding personal relationship with himself. He summons us decisively to live out our life of faith in the freedom of God's children.

In peak moments, our faith-renewal can become a radical decision for Christ. So far as we are able, we summon the fullness of our freedom for self-donation to our Lord. We commit ourselves to him and we bond ourselves with him. We pledge fidelity to Christ in our Christian vocation for the open-ended future so far as we can control it.

We can further renew our commitment to Christ's vision and values. Our fathers and mothers in the faith have passed down a traditional understanding of the cosmos that draws upon Gospel values. As we ourselves mature in our spirituality, we have the opportunity to claim the Catholic worldview as our own precious legacy. We then develop a Catholic mind that reflects the Church's attitudes and a Catholic conscience that is formed on the Church's teachings.

Our Commitment to the Church

Our Lord called his first disciples to follow him not singly but as members of a community. We Catholic Christians, therefore, are ecclesial Christians. As we decide to be Christ's disciples, we choose also to follow him in the company of all our fellow-disciples, whom he gathers together and among whom he abides. We relate to Christ and give ourselves to the Church by one and the same volition. Our connection with the Church, then, is not a dispensable afterthought, but a primary dimension of our relationship with Christ himself.

Christ is mysterious, and Christ's Church participates in his mystery. We access Christ with his Church only by faith. In Catholic spirituality, we believe into Christ, although he himself is a union of the divine and the human, and we cannot comprehend all that he is. We believe also into his Church, although she is a union of divinity with humanity, sanctity with sinfulness, and invisible life with visible structure, and we cannot grasp all that she is.

We can, of course, view the Church from a historical, comparative, and rationalist perspective. For example, we can study her objectively as one among many other world religions that possess analogous belief systems and moral codes, communal bonds, and cults of worship. We can analyze her sociologically and count her members, ordained clergy, Religious, churches, and institutions of health, education, and public welfare. We can calculate her historical impact anthropologically and culturally, philosophically and psychologically. But, for all of this, we would still fail to confront the internal reality of the Church as a *mystery* of God's grace. We can know the Risen Christ only by faith, and we can know Christ's Church only by faith.

Christ is unique and incomparable, and the Church he founded is also distinctive and unparalleled. We deliberately choose Jesus Christ and his Community, and we feel privileged to take part in Catholic life and worship. We gladly make our spiritual home within Christ's Church for the course of our lives, and no enticement can lead us to injure her, to betray her, or to abandon her.

We freely believe in Christ, our Lord and Savior, and therefore we deliberately believe in the Church that prolongs his presence in history and around the world. Christ is our Head, and the Church is his Body through which he is accessible. We, the members of the Church, are many, with diverse identities, gifts, and talents, yet we constitute a single community in a single communion. We appear on the surface, of course, to be millions of discrete and separate individuals, yet the Holy Spirit enlivens us collectively as one Body, with one Lord, one faith, and one baptism.

We freely adhere to Christ in faith, and therefore, we also cling to his Church, the community of faith. We gather together with women and men of every ethnicity and race, of every age and social status, and we aspire toward deeper unity in Christ. We are different persons of the most amazing diversity, yet we experience a common bond of extraordinary power. (As one insightful Catholic has put it about our tradition, "Here comes everybody!") We are indebted to one another; we are sisters and brothers, and we owe one another service and support; we are members of the same family, and we owe one another compassion and intercessory prayer.

We willingly hope in Christ, our Lord and Savior, and, therefore, we deliberately hope in the Church that mediates to us Christ's risen victory over death. We are the members

of Christ's bride who for now experience our collective sinfulness, but we hope finally to be purified from spot and
wrinkle and every other such thing when Christ returns in
glory. We suffer many dyings during our lives, of course, yet
the Holy Spirit purifies us in preparation for our definitive
passage from this world to resurrection with Christ.

We willingly love Christ, and therefore we deliberately love the Church that makes Christ accessible to us in
our time and place. Since the Church is Christ's bride, she
is also our mother, and we relate to her with filial fidelity.
Such devotion to the Church seems to be a unique feature
of Catholic spirituality. We speak readily of "Holy Mother
Church," and we refer to her in the feminine, because
we experience something unmistakably maternal about
her ministry to us (despite her patriarchal structures).
Consequently, we relate to one another as "daughters and
sons of the Church" in a single family.

Our devotion to the Church underscores the spirit of
Catholicism. We look to Holy Mother Church for her wisdom and for her counsel, for her strength and for her healing. We feed on saving truths from her teaching authority,
and we receive vital nourishment from her sacraments. We
weep for our Church when scandal wounds her, and we
work wholeheartedly for her reform (a recent example of
this has been a lay movement known as "The Voice of the
Faithful"). We defend our Church when she is attacked,
and we bear public witness to all that she means to us.

Indeed, every aspect of our Catholic life has an ecclesial dimension. Upon our baptism into Christ, for example, we enter our Christian community. Every time that we receive any sacrament, we relate to Christ, yes, but also to our Church in a new or renewed way. Every time we study sacred scripture, we steep ourselves in our community's book. Every time we reflect upon doctrine, we immerse ourselves in our community's Tradition. Every action we perform and every Christian goal that we achieve in Christ we accomplish as members of our Church. We spend our whole lives on our Church's pilgrimage back to the Father, and we are never alone.

Our Life of Faith Both to Will and to Accomplish

Jesus insists that we must live according to the faith that we confess: "Not everyone who says to me, 'Lord, Lord,' will enter the kingdom of heaven, but only the one who does the will of my Father in heaven" (Matthew 7:21). We betray our faith-commitment if we do not allow it to impact our everyday lives. Our practical performance must be in synch with our Christian vocation, vision, and values, or else we risk the scandal of hypocrisy and scandal. Our faith-commitment requires a volitional fidelity to the Lord on a daily basis, ever to be renewed, always to be deepened.

Our participation in the Holy Eucharist demands that we live out what we celebrate. When we gather at the altar for Holy Communion, we receive the Risen Christ and his saving grace toward an active and practical faith. The prayer after Communion for the Feast of St. Thomas the Apostle says it perfectly: "Father, in this sacrament we have received the body and blood of Christ. With Saint Thomas we acknowledge him to be our Lord and God. *May we show by our lives that our faith is real.* We ask this through Christ our Lord" (italics added). When the celebrant dismisses us at the conclusion of Mass, he often says, "Go forth to love and serve the world." He sends us forth to demonstrate what we believe by how we act.

We may falter occasionally, and we may grow weary often. Sometimes we may even become confused and lose our way. Yet we can pick up the pieces and begin again. Our participation in the Sacrament of Reconciliation requires that we repent of our sins and make a firm purpose of amendment for the future. In this way we sacramentalize what must be our ongoing experience: a daily turning away from our sins with a new turning toward the Lord. Catholic spirituality has always contained this conversionist rhythm.

Of course, our Christian life inevitably presents problems and challenges. To modify the famous words of M. Scott Peck, *Christian* "life is difficult." We confront many challenges along the way of life, but even life itself is a problem. By will power and the grace of God, however, we confidently take on the vicissitudes of life and we manage them. We overcome our temptations, we discipline our emotions, and we cope with our physical disabilities. God's grace fortifies our volition that we may persevere in our commitment until we complete our journey home.

> *Many persons have a wrong idea of what constitutes true happiness. It is not attained through self-gratification, but through fidelity to a worthy purpose.* (Helen Keller)

Toward Reflective Journaling

Faithful discipleship according to Christ's mind and heart requires that we respond in love and freedom to every person who enters our life.

QUESTIONS FOR DISCUSSION

1. What role does active resolve and renewed determination play in your spiritual life?

2. Have you ever experienced consciously the working of the Holy Spirit in your life—illuminating your mind with knowledge and inspiring your will with love and freedom?

Chapter Six

CHRISTIAN VITALITY

"For through the law I died to the law, so that I might live to God. I have been crucified with Christ; and it is no longer I who live, but it is Christ who lives in me. And the life I now live in the flesh I live by faith in the Son of God, who loved me and gave himself for me."
(Galatians 2:19–20)

A PROPHETIC MODEL OF CHRISTIAN VITALITY: DR. ALBERT SCHWEITZER

Dr. Albert Schweitzer would be a hard act for anyone to follow: A man of extraordinary gifts, he lived and labored by a remarkable vitality of Christ's Spirit. Very seldom did such a person emerge in our era and make so great a difference in the lives of so many. Only God knows the full extent and fruitfulness of Dr. Schweitzer's enormous labor as a healer in the tradition of his Master. Driven by deep faith and motivated by altruistic love, Dr. Schweitzer was brilliant in intellect, but he was also immensely compassionate in heart.

Albert Schweitzer was determined in will, but he was also marvelously creative in imagination. He cared deeply about the sufferings of humankind, but he also applied himself forcefully to the relief of their pain. Schweitzer was neither a Catholic nor an American, but he was undoubtedly a Christian who earned admiration internationally from believers and unbelievers alike. Nobody who knew his story was surprised when, in 1952, Dr. Schweitzer won the Nobel Prize for Peace.

A prodigious thinker, Schweitzer excelled not only as a Christian philosopher, theologian, and scripture scholar, but also as a professor, a preacher, and a biographer. Dr. Schweitzer achieved uncommon success as a student and professor at the University of Strasbourg, and his pivotal study *The Quest of the Historical Jesus* (1906) is still an assignment for biblical students. An accomplished artist, Schweitzer presented virtuoso performances as a concert organist and even designed organs himself. Albert Schweitzer loved the world of academe with its stimulating interchange with intellectuals, yet he needed to devote his gifts to the service of others.

When Dr. Schweitzer was thirty years old, he fulfilled his vow to dedicate himself to alleviating the sufferings of humankind. In his wisdom he once wrote, "Whoever is spared personal pain must feel himself called to help in diminishing the pain of others." Schweitzer studied medicine and then gave himself as a medical missionary to forty years of labor among the natives of French Equatorial Africa. He planned, built, and directed his own hospital.

Dr. Albert Schweitzer was a charismatic figure who actuated his talents, accomplished his dreams, and lived life to the very full. But he exceeded his scholarly credentials when he published his book *Reverence for Life*. Schweitzer had discovered through prayerful meditation and selfless service that God is Love, and that the highest purpose of human life was to love God and to care for one's fellow human beings.

Dr. Albert Schweitzer lived what he preached: "Humanitarianism consists in this that no man is to be sacrificed for some other end." Schweitzer certainly made a substantive difference for untold thousands of people, and he left this world a much better place for his having lived in it.

We shall long remember Dr. Albert Schweitzer as a Christian of monumental achievements. Most of all, however, we shall revere his memory as a vital servant of God for others. He advised us all: "Search and see if there is not some place where you can invest your humanity."

The Theme of Christian Vitality

Christian vitality is a sharing in the vitality of Christ himself, our new life in Christ. This *vitality* is a matter of "divine grace," an altogether new life that utterly surpasses the natural life that we receive from our parents. Jesus Christ came so that we might have his divine life and have it more abundantly. The Holy Spirit graces us with this life of God's children so that we may pray affectionately to our dear Father as *"Abba."*

On the natural level, we can understand "vitality" as a happy blend of inherited genes, training, environmental development, and personal history. Some of us possess vast resources of such vitality. Such people are the energetic activists, who are sometimes impetuous, usually enthusiastic, and always hardworking. They may simultaneously engage in many different projects while they make ample time for a vibrant social life. The less "vital" among us are the more taciturn contemplatives, who are sometimes cautious, usually reflective, and always measured in their response. Such people are happy to focus on one project at a time while they portion out their social life among a select circle of friends. Whether our natural temperament is exuberant or reserved, however, the Holy Spirit empowers us all to live in Christ with the vitality of God.

Our Christian vitality draws upon Jesus Christ and includes all the graces we need to live, to love, and to serve as disciples of Christ in the holy Church. St. Paul the Apostle teaches us to realize this: "So you must consider yourselves dead to sin and alive to God in Christ Jesus" (Rom. 6:10). Paul reminded the Colossians to persevere in so wondrous a life: "As you therefore have received Christ Jesus the Lord, continue to live in him, rooted and built up in him and established in the faith, just as you were taught, abounding in thanksgiving" (Col. 1:6). Christ is the Bread of Life, and we are the guests at his table. Christ is the Way, the Truth, and the Life, and our religion is a personal relationship with him. Christ is the Resurrection and the Life, and we participate in his Paschal Mystery. Christ is the living Vine, and we are the abiding branches that draw our vitality from him.

By grace, we abide in Christ, and Christ dwells within us. We live, now not we, but Christ lives in us. By grace, our fullest existence is Christ, and our self-abnegation is growth. By grace, we serve others in Christ, and we participate in his redemptive work. By grace, we continuously pass over from death to life in Christ, and we share in his victory. Indeed, the grace of Christ animates every dimension of our spirituality, and it is this that distinguishes our peculiarly Christian spirituality from all other religious experiences.

Catholic spirituality is all about Christ's gift of grace in the Spirit and our free involvement with that grace. We readily respect those nonbelievers who lead decent, ethical lives; after all, our own spirituality also requires that we lead lives of moral goodness. We also admire those devoted people who spend themselves in acts of generosity; after all, our own spirituality also demands that we serve others altruistically. Yet Catholic spirituality involves much more than strength of will and kindness of heart.

Our spirituality results from the primacy of Christ's grace over us but not without our free response. It concerns the new life and the marvelous activity that Christ effects within us by his Holy Spirit. We receive natural energy from our food, oxygen, and exercise, but Christ enables us to share in his salvific action for the redemption of the world. Christian vitality involves our personal self-transcendence and transformation, whether or not we experience those gifts in any felt way.

We can rejoice in St. Paul's beautiful prayer: "I pray that, according to the riches of his glory, he may grant that you may be strengthened in your inner being with power through his Spirit, and that Christ may dwell in your hearts through faith, as you are being rooted and grounded in love" (Eph. 3:16–17). The Risen Christ dwells within us to invigorate every aspect of our spirituality, from our initial vocation as disciples to our Christian vision, values, voice, volition, and virtues. Christ's Holy Spirit activates our potential for faithful and energetic discipleship.

Christian vitality empowers us to overcome vicissitudes so that we may complete our journey to the Father. Grace charges our spirituality with motive power so that we may sustain our spirituality with forward thrust. Grace revives us when we are weary so that we may overcome ennui and burnout.

Christ's vitality enlightens our minds not only that we may believe but also that we may realize the lifestyle that faith demands. Grace expands our faith with depth of commitment, even when we confront torturous doubt. Christ's vitality inspires our hearts not only that we may hope in Christ but also that we may finally achieve the higher goals that hope requires. Grace supports our hope with steadfast endurance, even when we suffer frustration and disappointment.

Above all, Christ's vitality inflames our being not only that we may love but also that we may become a loving person as Christ is. Grace provides us with the stamina we need for selfless service of others over the long haul, even when we receive only rejection in return. Christ's vitality fortifies us for continued loving, even when we must confront obstacles and hardships, mental setbacks, and physical ills.

Christ's vitality, therefore, elevates us not only to action by sublime moral norms but also to life at a *super*natural level as adoptive sons and daughters in Christ's natural Sonship. Grace drives us toward the heights of holiness where Christ is enthroned as Lord of glory. Indeed, some of us may occasionally even enjoy privileged moments when grace floods our being with sentiments of fervent praise and thanksgiving for all that our God is for us.

In this chapter we shall consider Christian vitality from three perspectives: (1) our sacramental life, (2) our communion of life with Mary and the saints, and (3) our life of hope.

Our Sacramental Life

The sacramental principle flows from the historical Incarnation of God's eternal Word among us. It affirms that God mediates his redemptive love through the glorified humanity of Jesus, and Jesus channels himself through his Church, through the ordained ministers of his Church, and through the seven Sacraments of his Church. Because of the principle of sacramentality, we can discern the saving presence of Christ in human interaction, and we can distinguish spiritual reality in the material. By sacramentality, we can access our Savior through material symbol by our bodily senses of sight, hearing, taste, smell, and touch.

Indeed, the sacramental principle affirms that we receive divine grace in and through the symbolic. Our powerful Lord is always the primary minister of the Sacraments—he remains alive and available to act upon us through them. Christ personally baptizes and confirms us. He personally absolves us from our postbaptismal sins through sacramental reconciliation. He personally binds bride and groom together in marriage. Christ personally ordains sacred ministers to represent him in his Church. He personally consecrates the seriously ill through the anointing of the sick.

We can absolutely depend upon this wondrous truth, even if an ordained minister were to appear unworthy. As St. Augustine once wrote, "Whether Peter baptizes or Judas baptizes, Christ baptizes." Therefore, our sacraments are infallibly efficacious signs of sacred events; they always effect what they signify, and they signify by effecting.

Of course, we have to watch out for the occupational

hazards of all sacramental practice. Externalism, irreverence, and mechanical repetition may reduce our sacred rituals to empty ritualism. We cannot forget that our reception of a sacrament is not merely the use of some sacred thing. Rather, every sacramental event opens up to an interactive encounter with Jesus Christ. Consequently, we have to approach each sacramental experience with the heightened consciousness of personalist faith and a receptive heart.

Here we confront a distinctive dimension of Catholic spirituality. As a matter of fact, we never do anything more typically Catholic than when we celebrate Christ's seven Sacraments and our Church's many sacramentals. Our sacramental activity first binds us to the ecclesial Body of Christ and then, only through that connection, unites us to Christ the head. Whereas many other Christians first go to Christ directly and only afterward gather together with other believers who know the Lord, we Catholics (and also Orthodox Christians) relate to Christ always through our Church, in communion with our Church, and never apart from the Church.

Our Church is itself the historical Sacrament or sign of Christ through which the unseen Lord acts upon us and through which we encounter him. If we give ourselves over to our new life in Christ, nonbelievers ought to be able to meet Christ in us and through us. That is why our scandals are not only a terrible sin against God, but also a violent wound inflicted upon our community. Even though we are all sinners who fall short of our vocation, we still remain members of Christ's holy Body, called to holiness and destined for final purification when our Lord returns in glory.

Each of us can draw upon Christ's vitality when we encounter Christ at many levels of ecclesial experience. Our Lord is present where two or three gather in his name, and he binds us together in a vital communion. He leads us communally in prayer and worship of the Father. He teaches us communally through his proclaimed Word at the sacred liturgy. We can discover Christ particularly in the poor, the needy, and the outcast. We have Christ's own promise of unbroken presence: "And remember, I am with you always, to the end of the age" (Matt. 28:20b).

We also meet our Lord through dozens of our Church's sacramentals. Sacramentals are symbols that resemble the sacraments and extend them in order to gather the whole of human life into the redemptive process. They sacralize human words such as special blessings for married couples, homes, and women in childbirth. They utilize earthly elements such as water, salt, candles, and oils. They consecrate sacred objects such as altars, holy seasons, and sacred places such as churches for worship.

Our Communion of Life with Mary and the Saints

In the great creeds of our Tradition, we acknowledge our shared vitality in Christ through the Communion of

Saints. This doctrine has long made a mighty impact upon our culture and upon our devotional practices. The wonderful truth is that Christ's Spirit binds all of us together in a single flow of divine life within one Body—invisibly and mysteriously, yes, but nonetheless redemptively, continuously, and in all reality. We need never feel alone as we struggle toward fidelity in discipleship. We can call upon the resources of a vast company as we pursue our own pilgrimage to the Father. We enjoy the encouragement, the prayers, and the caring support of countless other women and men who are walking or have walked with us on the same journey.

Of course, we especially cultivate a devout and loving relationship with Christ's mother, the most blessed, ever-virgin Mary. We venerate Mary liturgically and privately as the preeminent member of our Church; she is the queen of all saints. We revere Mary as the perfectly redeemed one; she was immaculately conceived at the beginning of her life, and she was gloriously assumed into heaven upon her life's earthly conclusion. We honor Mary as the spouse of the Holy Spirit and the seat of wisdom. Most of all, we commune with Mary, the mother of God, and we implore her intercession as truly *our* mother.

Within the Communion of Saints, we also celebrate our shared vitality in Christ with the whole Church triumphant, that is, with all the celestial hosts of saints who already enjoy the beatific vision of God. We take delight in their marvelous achievements while in this world. We typically have our favorites such as St. Peter and St. Thomas Aquinas, St. Theresa of Avila and St. Therese of Lisieux, but we feel personal devotion to many more. We remember our saints universally in the liturgy, we acknowledge their accessibility to us in Christ, and we beseech their intercession on our behalf. We study the lives of our saints, and we emulate them as models of Christian discipleship. We revere the saints as God's masterpieces of grace, and we praise our God who has transformed them in Christ: "Blessed be God, in his angels and in his saints."

We rejoice in the Communion of Saints as our sanctifying bond with God's holy ones, persons who have superbly exemplified the myriad aspects of the Christian life in all its concreteness. We recognize their personal availability in Christ, and we cherish their friendship. We seek the patronage of our saints, and we communicate with them. We can confidently ask them to pray for us through Christ.

In Catholic spirituality, we also celebrate our communion in Christ with the Church suffering, that is, with all the departed persons who somehow experience necessary purification as they prepare for heaven. Union with our loved ones endures despite our apparent separation by death, because the grace of Christ continues to bind us together. We gather to thank God for their lives in the Mass of the Resurrection. It is a significant part of our Holy Tradition that we remember all the persons in Purgatory.

We feel closely bound to them, we feel compassionate love for them, and we pray for them both in the liturgy and in our private devotions. We even devote the whole month of November to praying for them.

Our Life of Hope

When we share in Christ's vitality, the Holy Spirit empowers us to relate to God by the "theological virtues" of faith, hope, and charity. In the Spirit's gift of Christian faith, we embrace God's self-revelation through Christ. In the Spirit's gift of Christian charity, we participate in God's love through Christ. In the Spirit's gift of Christian hope, we fasten upon God's fidelity through Christ. We can conquer fear and be steadfast, because we trust in God's faithful power. We can dispel anxiety over our sinfulness, because we can count upon God's faithful mercy. We can be resolute in renewed conversion, because we rely upon God's faithful love. We lift our eyes to God's fidelity, because God always raises the dead.

God has vindicated the divine faithfulness throughout the history of salvation. The aged Abraham and Sarah went through death to life, when God made them the parents of Isaac. Moses and the Israelites went through death to life, when God led them out of slavery in Egypt. The Jews of the Babylonian captivity went through death to life, when God led them back to their homeland. Above all, Jesus Christ went through death to life, when God raised him to resurrected life.

Jesus Christ conquered Satan, sin, and death by his Paschal Mystery: his passage through crucifixion into glorious resurrected life. We who have faith in Christ have been baptized into his death and Resurrection, and we belong to him. We who know Christ celebrate his death and Resurrection in the Holy Eucharist, and we regularly remember him. We who cling to Christ share in his victory over death, and we continuously pass over with him. Christ's Passage provides the power and the momentum of our spirituality. So we hope. People often observe that where there's life, there's hope. The reverse is also true; where there's hope, there's life!

If I considered death at all in my younger days, I thought of it as something very remote—a single event of the body that mostly old people endured. Now that I am older, however, I have come to realize that we many times experience death of mind, spirit, or body. It is surely an important consequence of our spirituality that we should learn in Christian vitality always to confront our myriad deaths with hope.

Animals die just once, but we human beings can die many times and in a variety of ways before our hearts stop beating. We die when we sin, for example, and we die when we are sinned against. We die when we fail at a project we hold dear, and we die when we suffer rejection. We die when we endure critical illness, and we die when we must bury those whom we love. Most of all, we die when we suffer heartbreak.

Yet we hope in the risen Christ who is Son-of-God in power. This is not a question of being temperamentally optimistic and upbeat or strong-willed and determined. Even less is it a matter of denying our pains and sufferings in Pollyanna fantasy. When we hope in Christ, we shoulder our cross in union with him, and we share in his victorious vitality. When we hope in Christ, we receive forgiveness for our sins, healing for our disabilities, and encouragement for new beginnings. When we hope in Christ, we can stand up and go forward again with renewed confidence in our future. When we hope in Christ, we can draw on the power we need in order to pass through death and rise again as a transformed person.

Julian of Norwich wrote: "All will be well and all manner of things will be well." Despite calamity, sickness, disappointment, and personal grief, we continue to hope that God has not abandoned us and will not do so. We are a loved people, and no sins are so terrible that they exceed God's mercy. God never casts us aside. Beyond the horrors of war, the brutality of injustice, and the terror of natural calamity, we maintain our hope that God's power can overcome all the evil in this world. Our God is merciful Love absolutely speaking, and our God is good enough, wise enough, and powerful enough always to bring greater good out of evil.

However overwhelming the poverty in our cities, the

misery of displaced persons, the tragedies of war and fam-
ine, and the oppression of the most vulnerable, we solidly
trust that this is not meant to be. We realize that such
horrors are not the result of blind fate, and that in God's
providence better things can always happen. Christian
hope demands that we work for the peace and justice of
the kingdom of God.

Today we have a whole industry of mental health pro-
fessionals working to alleviate guilt, aid wounded psyches,
and repair the excesses of our personal lives. Many people
are so scarred by their past sins that their lives are paralyzed.
We in the Christian Community can send out a bedrock
message: hope in the Risen Christ.

Whatever our challenges, Christian hope gives us a
sense of purpose through them all. Our hope drives out all
fear, because we know that we can be forgiven and we can
delete all our sins from memory. Our hope eliminates all
doubt, because we are certain that we live in the embrace of
Christ, and Christ will not let us go. Our hope bears fruit
in a wondrous, all-pervasive peace, because of our unshakable conviction; steeped in God's merciful love we live, and
move, and have our being.

> *We do not want you to be unaware, brothers and sis-*
> *ters, of the affliction we experienced in Asia; for we were*
> *so utterly unbearably crushed that we despaired of life*
> *itself. Indeed, we felt that we had received the sentence of*

death so that we would rely not on ourselves but on God
who raises the dead. (2 Cor. 1:8–9)

Toward Reflective Journaling

Faithful discipleship according to Christ's vitality requires that we live in continual openness to the Holy Spirit.

QUESTIONS FOR DISCUSSION

1. Do you understand the link between learning to love more selflessly and entering life more abundantly?

2. Have you ever experienced the truth of Christ's teaching that those who seek their life will lose it, while those who lose their life will find it?

Chapter Seven

CHRISTIAN VIRTUE

"As the Father has loved me, so I have loved you; abide in my love. If you keep my commandments, you will abide in my love, just as I have kept my Father's command- ments and abide in his love. I have said these things to you so that my joy may be in you, and that your joy may be complete. This is my commandment that you love one another as I have loved you." (John 15:9–12)

A PROPHETIC MODEL OF CHRISTIAN VIRTUE: MOTHER TERESA OF CALCUTTA

In the Catholic Tradition, we make much of our canon- ized saints: those faithful disciples of Christ who have led graced lives of heroic virtue. In our own time, Catholics around the world have spontaneously acclaimed the saint- hood of Mother Teresa of Calcutta (1910–97), the strong- willed "saint of the gutters." When we review the saints for our times, Mother Teresa may be the first person of whom we think. We have loved her, and we have been so proud of her because of her extraordinary love.

Indeed, Mother Teresa of Calcutta has won the admi- ration of believers and nonbelievers alike. If there is anyone from our contemporary world who has reflected divine love, it has surely been this diminutive sister in the one dollar white sari with the blue trim. Servant of the helpless, healer of the sick, comforter of the dying, beacon of joy and peace, prophet of Christ's compassion for the poor, Mother Teresa has modeled the power of love for a scarred and violent world. The very mention of her name has inspired millions of us to want to be more like her.

Over fifty years ago, Mother Teresa had discovered a woman "half eaten by maggots and rats" lying on the street in devastating misery. She remained by the poor person's side until her death. She then established a home where human beings could experience merciful love and conclude their lives with a sense of their own self-worth. Mother Teresa was a charismatic leader, and many others soon joined her in this quintessential work of compassion. She founded a new Religious congregation, the Missionaries of Charity, which now includes more than four thousand members, who serve the needy in over one hundred countries. Since then she has originated a worldwide network of shelters for the sick, the abandoned, and the dying poor.

Mother Teresa was a self-effacing person of Christlike *humility*, who had learned from Jesus to be meek and humble of heart. She sought no worldly reward or acclaim, and she steadfastly avoided the limelight. She gave herself personally and totally to each individual in her care so that she could create "something beautiful for God." Even when she received the Nobel Peace Prize in 1979, she diverted the spotlight from herself to the poverty-stricken millions for whom she labored. She stated simply: "I am grateful to receive [the Nobel Prize] in the name of the hungry, the naked, the homeless, of the crippled, of the blind, of the lepers, of all those people who feel unwanted, unloved, uncared-for throughout society, people that have become a burden to the society and are shunned by everyone."

Mother Teresa was a determined person of Christlike *fortitude*, who fearlessly entered a world of horrendous suffering and embraced the wretched poverty of those whom she served. She bravely sought mercy for the disenfranchised, the oppressed, and the marginalized whom society failed to acknowledge. She boldly ministered to the weak and the defenseless whom society ignored. She courageously cared for the helpless and the forsaken whom the world forgot. Indeed, Mother Teresa cried out for social justice on behalf of Christ and for the sake of the silent millions who suffer grinding, dehumanizing poverty.

Mother Teresa was a prophetic person of Christlike *reverence* for human life, however weakened, however aged, however ravaged by disease. She recognized the image of God in every human being without exception. She longed to make the forsaken realize their personal dignity as God's beloved and cherished children. Mother Teresa labored to fill the destitute with a sense of self-esteem despite the devastation of their wounds, the corruption of their flesh, or the imminence of their death.

Mother Teresa gathered the dying from the gutters and made them feel valued if only for a few moments during their last days. She bore witness to her vision of faith: "When I wash the leper's wounds, I feel I am nursing the Lord himself." She insisted that every child has a God-given right to pursue a happy life free of poverty, and she defended the lives of the unborn. She protested against abortion as the rejection of God's gift: "If you do not want him, give him to me."

Above all, Mother Teresa was a person of Christian *love*, who acquired so many virtues precisely because she loved so much. She reached out in every direction to embrace the unloved. She was frail and sometimes sickly, yet her powerful love made an unforgettable impact upon the contemporary world. Mother Teresa gave herself daily to the hopelessly lonely and the destitute, feeding the hungry, bathing the sick, and comforting the dying. She recognized the countenance of Christ on the tortured faces of the desperately suffering, despite Christ's "distressing disguise."

Mother Teresa demonstrated before the world that Christian love is not self-indulgent but sacrificial, not mechanical but revolutionary, not sentimental but stronger than death. She proved that uncalculated service, disinterested care, and altruistic dedication to others are truly possible in our self-serving world and not just impractical dreams void of substance. Mother Teresa by her life exemplified the revolutionary power of unconditional love.

The Theme of Christian Virtue

Our Catholic spirituality must above all flow from our sharing in Christ's virtue of divine *Agape* ("selfless, unconditional love"). Christ's love is that supreme gift of grace that the Holy Spirit pours forth within our hearts, enabling us also to love. Our Christian virtue of charity draws upon Christ's love, and it moves into eternity beyond faith and hope as the greatest of virtues. Our Christian virtue fulfills Christ's new commandment and covers a multitude of sins. We have to open up to Christ's love so that we may learn to love mercifully with his love and love indiscriminately as he loves. Christ's love must characterize our lives and inspire all our actions so that people may know that we are Christ's disciples.

Every religious tradition challenges its adherents to attain one supreme virtue that crowns all the others and gives them their deepest meaning. For example, Jews fasten upon the virtue of *tzedakah* ("justice") as they follow the way of the holy *Torah.* Muslims pursue the virtue of *taqwa* ("pious righteousness") as they adhere to the straight path of the holy *Quran.* Southern Buddhists seek the virtue of *bodhi* ("wisdom") while Northern Buddhists develop the virtue of *karuna* ("compassion") as they practice the Middle Way of the Buddha.

In *Agape*-love we spontaneously intend not our own fulfillment for our own sake, but the fulfillment of others for their sake. We become women and men of Christ's

Agape-love insofar as we are faithful to our vocation, vision, values, and volition. We become persons of Christ's *Agape*-love insofar as we channel to others the divine love that we have received. We become disciples of Christ's *Agape*-love insofar as we become truly benevolent toward all others, disinterestedly, altruistically, and seeking no return.

In our authentic Catholic Tradition, we have always preferred a morality based upon the positive acquisition of *Agape*-love. Our ethical life ought to spring not from a servile fear of doing what is wrong, but from the loving commitment to do what is right. We need not to avoid what is legally prohibited, but to fulfill what love requires. We should live not by multiple constraints, but by the spontaneous direction of an inner-directed conscience. Even our Sunday Mass obligation simply disciplines us toward that maturity whereby we long freely out of love to gather at the altar.

True, we are sinners who frequently fail to love as we should. Jesus taught that the just man falls seventy times seven times a day. We readily claim the Church of sinners as our spiritual home. We try to love, but self-interestedly and only from time to time. We attempt to love, but partially and only selectively. We will to love, but inconstantly and only when it meets our convenience.

We must often confess our infidelities. We must always struggle to overcome our weaknesses, and we must daily repent for our transgressions. We must plead in the Lord's Prayer for God's forgiveness and for God's deliverance from temptation. We cannot celebrate holy Mass without our communal plea for mercy, and we cannot approach the Communion table without our joint protest of unworthiness.

Despite our shortcomings, however, we retain our basic goodness as God's created image, and we share in Christ's *Agape*-love as God's graced children. Our graced discipleship leads beyond moral rectitude to inner transformation by love. Our graced discipleship is a process of growth beyond "leading a good life"into the heart of Christ. Through Christ, with Christ, and in Christ, we become fully human insofar as we become virtuous persons of *Agape*-love.

Our sharing in Christ's virtue of *Agape*-love engenders a fruitful spirituality. *Agape* heals our weaknesses and restores our wholeness. *Agape* structures our character and orders us toward successful humanity. *Agape* facilitates effective prayer and empowers our witness. Our participation in Christ's virtue of *Agape* validates our identity as disciples of *Agape*-incarnate.

In this chapter we shall consider this critically important theme of Christian virtue from three perspectives: (1) our God is *Agape*-love (2) Our Lord, the embodiment of God's *Agape*-love, and (3) our life of *Agape*-love.

Our God is Agape-*love*

In classical Greek literature we find several words that

denote the varieties of human "love." They wrote of *eros* ("love of desire"), of *storge* ("love of familial affection"), and of *philia* ("love of friendship"). There was a fourth Greek word that occurred only rarely, however: *Agape* ("spiritual love of altruistic benevolence"). Yet the word *Agape* with its verbal variants recurs repeatedly as the term of choice among New Testament authors. Jesus by his teachings, his works, and his very life had revealed an ideal of selfless beneficence so revolutionary that no other Greek word could do it justice.

At the heart and core of our faith, therefore, we must affirm that God is an incomprehensible mystery of *Agape*-love. By our human standards, we find God's *Agape*-love to be immoderate, excessive, and unreasonable. Nevertheless, we must believe that our God is *Agape*-love without further qualification. Our God, the true God, transcends all our concepts and surpasses our understanding. In this case, what sounds "too good to be true" actually is!

We have to struggle vigorously in order to accept the revelation of God's *Agape* through Jesus' crucifixion. When we gaze upon the Cross, the power of God's *Agape* shocks us as weakness, the mercy of God's *Agape* scandalizes us as undeserved forgiveness, and the wisdom of God's *Agape* puzzles us as utter foolishness. We cannot understand God's love, yet we cling unhesitatingly to the image of Jesus dying on the crucifix as the decisive confirmation of our faith.

Agape-love implies personal relationality, and the mysterious inner life of our God is a communion among the three Persons of the Blessed Trinity. The Father is the Lover, the Son is the Loved One, and the Holy Spirit is the subsistent Love between the Father and the Son. The Father *generates* ("begets") his Son and communicates the fullness of divinity to him; in their mutual embrace, the Father and the Son together *spirate* ("breathe forth") the Holy Spirit.

Agape-love is also God's supreme motive in all that God does. Our God created all things in heaven and on earth out of *Agape*-love for us. That is why every creature must retain always its reflection of God's truth, goodness, and beauty. Our God revealed God's own self to us out of *Agape*-love for us. After all, we do not disclose ourselves to those whom we do not love. God's Revelation also unveils God's magnificent plan of *Agape* for us: to restore all things in Christ. Indeed, God redeemed us out of *Agape*-love: "For God so loved the world that he gave his only Son, so that everyone who believes in him may not perish but may have eternal life" (John 3:16).

Our Christian spirituality must rest solidly upon the fundamental truth that God is Love. All of our reflections upon God should begin from here and find their guiding parameters here. All of our theological questioning about God and God's ways must find its generative principle here. When our inquiries lead us only to impenetrable mystery that transcends our understanding, we can only bow our heads and observe, "In the end, it is a matter of love. *Agape* is like that; *Agape* does such things."

Once we fully accept God's wondrous *Agape*, we can leave behind all destructive fears and anxieties. For then we know that no number of human beings can exhaust God's concern, and no depths of sinfulness can challenge God's mercy. But we must wholeheartedly believe into God's love as being really real. We have to believe into God's *Agape* unreservedly, trust in it unfailingly, and depend upon it unswervingly.

Jesus warned us that we must return to our open confidence as children if we are to accept God's Love: "Let the little children come to me, and do not stop them; for it is to such as these that the kingdom of God belongs. Truly I tell you, whoever does not receive the kingdom of God as a little child will never enter it'"(Luke 18:16-17). We may have to convert from our rationalistic assumptions and sophisticated criticism. We may need to discard all those false deities of our presumptive invention and cling to the one true God. We must return to the boldness of children before their "Daddy," who, they know, can refuse them nothing. Here the observation of St. Theresa of Avila is pertinent: "Prayer is communion between ourselves and the God by whom we are absolutely confident that we are loved."

Our Lord, the Embodiment of God's Agape-love

Jesus Christ is the Father's gift of *Agape* incarnate for us and for our salvation. In our Savior, we discover God's *Agape* humanly enfleshed, humanly interpreted, and humanly expressed. Jesus demonstrated God's *Agape* by all that he did and said. Those who encountered our Lord gazed upon divinity knowing them through human eyes, heard divinity teaching them through a human voice, and felt divinity touching them through human hands. The poor, the sinners, and the marginalized responded with joy in the knowledge that God loved them. But Jesus demonstrated God's *Agape* most of all by his suffering and death on the Cross: "But God proves his love for us in that while we still were sinners Christ died for us" (Rom. 5:8).

As the ideal human being, Jesus Christ also embodies the perfection of every other ideal and virtue in *Agape*-love. Christ is our ultimate criterion for the true, our enduring norm for the good, and our personal exemplar for the beautiful. That is why Catholic spirituality must always remain Christocentric in its core and orientation.

Christ is our master who calls us to follow him, but he is also our faithful companion who abides within us on our journey. Christ is our teacher who exhorts us to love, but he is also our friend who empowers us for loving. Christ is our model who inspires us to pursue Christian virtue, but he is also our Lord who gives us the Spirit to energize us both to will and to accomplish.

In our pursuit of discipleship, therefore, we do not merely foster the so-called "cardinal virtues" of the philosophers—justice, fortitude, temperance, and prudence.

We reflect upon Christ's teachings in order to take on his vision and prioritize his values in our own lives. We study all that we can learn of Christ's earthly life so that we may emulate him in his relations with others. We do not merely imitate Christ's gestures or mimic his style of speech; we seek to empty ourselves that his presence may fill us. We share ever more deeply in Christ's *Agape*-love so that we may relate to God as our dear *Abba*, to every woman as our sister, and to every man as our brother.

Christ fortifies our lives, inspiring them with noble purpose and substantive meaning. He illuminates our minds, actively instructing us throughout our lifetime. Christ encourages our hearts, accompanying us daily at every step. He directs our hands, working through our ministry to the needy. Christ guides our feet, counseling us toward right choices. He abides within us and among us as we move from our constrained egocentricity to the freedom of selfless service.

Our Life of Agape-*Love*

Christ made our mandate to love unequivocal when he quoted the Old Testament approvingly: "He said to him, 'You shall love the Lord your God with all your heart, and with all your soul, and with all your mind.' This is the greatest and first commandment. And a second is like it: 'You shall love your neighbor as yourself.' On these two commandments hang all the law and the prophets" (Matt. 22:37-40). At the Last Supper, however, Jesus summed up our whole necessity of loving with a single commandment: "I give you a new commandment, that you love one another. Just as I have loved you, you also should love one another" (John 13:34). We might have expected Jesus to tell us to love *him* as he had loved us. For Jesus, it was clear that our love for one another would at once involve us in the total love of our God.

As Christian disciples, we have been made to know that God loves us, and so we are bound to communicate that love in unmistakable terms to our sisters and brothers. We must pass forward what we have received, proclaiming the good news by word and deed. God's *Agape* is invisible, of course, but we can make it palpably accessible by our disinterested service.

Without God's special assistance, it would be impossible for us human beings ever to love with *Agape*. God gives us a sharing in the divine *Agape* that expanded the heart of Christ. Our participation in Christ's *Agape* is God's gift to us, a grace that we can neither earn nor deserve. Progressing under the impact of God's love, we learn to love with God's love. Our sharing in Christ's *Agape* endures within our hearts as our foremost virtue: "And now faith, hope, and love abide, these three; and the greatest of these is love" (1 Cor. 13:13).

Agape-love amounts to our free benevolence toward others, and it can be surprisingly dispassionate. The virtue of *Agape*-love is more than sentiment, warm affection, emotion, or even passionate engagement, although these feelings may accompany our love and they sometimes result from it. Most of us do not experience any affection in our love for God, since supernatural *Agape* is qualitatively different from natural *eros*, *storge*, and *philia*. We need not worry if we honestly recognize that we *feel* more attachment to members of our family. We may "feel" nothing in our love for God, yet our love is authentic if we want to fulfill God's holy will and we can pray sincerely: "Thy will be done."

Agape purifies our motivation and energizes our activities with the highest purpose that we human beings may conceive. By God's grace we can even have *Agape* for someone whom we dislike, even a mean and cruel individual who remains truly detestable. The critical question is, do we freely *will* what is good for that person? Do we earnestly pray for those who hurt us, do we sincerely want what is best for those who hate us?

Agape-love includes all the other virtues within itself. If we faithfully love God and neighbor, we shall surely be just, prudent, temperate, and courageous. If we become loving persons, we shall inevitably be patient and kind, truthful and honest, humble and generous. *Agape*-love liberates us to lead a virtuous life free of external pressure and internal constraint. As St. Augustine once remarked about Christian loving in freedom, "Love God and do what you will."

Because God has endowed us with free will, we can

meet the most stringent criterion for genuine success as human beings. We can become *loving persons*. We can opt fundamentally for the welfare of all human beings. We can love the partial reflections of our God in God's creatures. We can harbor goodwill toward all people, we can serve them seeking no return, and we can embrace them in compassionate concern.

Of course, we must discipline our instinctive impulses to like or dislike individuals because of qualities we find winsome or abrasive and obnoxious. We naturally find some people to be attractive while we find some other people to be disagreeable. We can experience instant "bad chemistry" with certain persons for no particular reason. But this is not an ethical issue, and we are not morally responsible for how we *feel* about people. We need to reject the evil that some people do, but we need not harbor bad will toward *them*.

We truly love when we decide to love others with *Agape*. We love when we act kindly, share generously, and care compassionately for others. We love when we attend to people's words and ponder people's thoughts. We love when we place the needs and concerns of others before our own. We love when we promote their peace and contentment. Most important, the Holy Spirit graces all of these human efforts so that our love participates in Christ's virtue: *Agape-love*.

Agape-love demands service of others before ourselves,

but we may find such generosity to be too costly. *Agape*-love demands denial of self as we take up our cross and follow Jesus, but we may find such austerity to be painful and distasteful. As Father Zossima insists in Dostoevsky's classic *Brothers Karamazov*, love in reality differs from love in dreams, because love in action is a harsh and dreadful thing. Yet *Agape*-love characterizes our Christian discipleship as nothing else does.

Over the course of a lifetime (and longevity is a blessing that extends our training), we must gradually learn to love both God and our fellow human beings by this supernal power. We can by God's grace become well disposed toward all people, seeking no compensation or reward. We can learn to plead to God for the welfare of all people, whether they like us or not. Finally, we can from our hearts forgive those who injure us, and we can ask forgiveness of those whom we have hurt. We can let go of resentments, we can defuse hostilities, and we can heal alienations. We can provide for the needy not only from our superfluity, but even from our substance. We can promote justice and peace in the world.

We can do the right thing in freedom from external laws, because we spontaneously follow the inner dictates of love. We can work for the fulfillment of others unreservedly, not because we find them lovable but because God has made them lovable in themselves. Jesus taught that our standard could not possibly be higher: "But love your enemies, do good and lend, expecting nothing in return. Your reward will be great, and you will be children of the Most High; for he is kind to the ungrateful and the wicked. Be merciful, just as your father is merciful'" (Luke 6:35-36).

Toward Reflective Journaling

Faithful discipleship according to Christ's mind and heart requires that we die daily to inordinate self-love and gradually learn to love others selflessly.

QUESTIONS FOR DISCUSSION

1.   How would you articulate the principal difference between *Agape*-love and other legitimate human loves such as those of familial affection, friendship, and desire?

2.   How should *Agape*-love govern all our other virtues, rules, and obligations?

Chapter Eight

CHRISTIAN VOYAGE

When he had seated himself with them to eat, he took bread, pronounced the blessing, then broke the bread and began to distribute it to them. With that their eyes were opened and they recognized him; whereupon he vanished from their sight. They said to one another, "Were not our hearts burning inside us as he talked to us on the road and explained the Scripture to us?" (Luke 24:30–32)

A PROPHETIC MODEL OF CHRISTIAN VOYAGE: ST. AUGUSTINE OF HIPPO (354–430)

St. Augustine of Hippo was far and away the most influential thinker in Church history, and his profound impact upon the Catholic Tradition continues until now. Together with St. Ambrose, St. Jerome, and St. Gregory the Great, St. Augustine is one of the four great Latin doctors of the Church. Bishop and mystic, philosopher and theologian, preacher and writer, St. Augustine produced countless sermons, treatises, and books. All of us in western Christianity bear an Augustinian stamp upon our religious consciousness.

St. Augustine contributed a rich and insightful theology of the Blessed Trinity through his struggle with the Arians. He plumbed the mystery of the Church and the Sacraments through his controversy with the Donatists. He earned the title "Doctor of Grace" because of his pioneering work against Pelagius. St. Augustine's most influential work, however, has surely been his autobiography, the *Confessions*, in which he cries out, "Too late have I loved thee, O Beauty ever ancient, ever new! Too late have I loved thee." Touching the hearts of all people of all ages, the *Confessions* is still unrivaled as the premier classic of all Christian literature.

In his *Confessions*, St. Augustine describes his personal voyage to Catholicism as a grand quest, a spiritual pilgrimage into the embrace of God. After his conversion, Augustine rejoiced with thanksgiving as he discerned how God had been working constantly through the people, relationships, places, and conflicts of his experience.

Often St. Augustine had felt himself far from God, but God was never far from him. In his hunger for divine truth, Augustine had experimented with the religious conviction of the Manichaeans and the philosophical skepticism of the Academics, with the folly of the Astrologists and the wisdom of the neo-Platonists. In Augustine's thirst for divine love, he had vainly pursued sexual pleasure and worldly acclaim. He had even traveled from Tagaste to Carthage, from Carthage to Rome, and from Rome to Milan.

St. Augustine found God most of all through the special people in his life. St. Monica, his Catholic mother, taught him early to reverence the sweet name of Jesus, and, despite years of sinful abandon, St. Augustine never lost his veneration for the Lord. Cicero's book *Hortensius* stimulated St. Augustine's desire for speculative truth. Alypius, a constant companion, taught Augustine about love of friendship. "Una," Augustine's mistress for many years, delivered herself to him in love of desire. Adeodatus, son of Augustine, introduced him to the love of familial affection.

The neo-Platonists led Augustine to conceive of God as purely spiritual and beyond the corporeal. The converted intellectual Victorinus provided Augustine with the example of courageous fidelity to conscience. St. Ambrose of Milan taught Augustine how to make sense of Scripture by means of allegorical interpretation. St. Athanasius's *Life of Antony* opened the young Augustine to the discipline of asceticism and celibate chastity. Finally, St. Paul's epistle to the Romans (13:13) inspired Augustine to make no allowance for his flesh but to surrender wholeheartedly to Christ.

The Theme of Christian Voyage

The theme of spiritual voyage has long been a privileged metaphor for the human condition. Our literary heroes and heroines have been people on a solemn quest for a more abundant life. Our classics include Homer's *Odyssey* and Virgil's *Aenead,* for example, together with Dante's *Divine Comedy* and Cervantes's *Don Quixote.*

The sacred journey for life also holds central place in the great religious traditions of the world. We think of the obligatory *hajj* to Mecca in Islam, for instance, and the immense popularity of pilgrimages in Hinduism and Buddhism. The Jews annually celebrate the pilgrimage feast of the Passover, because their exodus from Egyptian slavery to covenanted nationhood constitutes their very identity as God's holy people.

Jesus Christ is the New Moses, the great wayfarer who broke through our human estrangement from God by his exodus from this world into the Father's bosom. Jesus became our redeemer by his Passage through death into Resurrection: "Now before the festival of the Passover, Jesus knew that his hour had come to depart from this world and go to the Father. Having loved his own who were in the world, he loved them to the end" (John 13:1). Completing his own journey through the Cross to glory, Jesus became in his own person the way for his disciples to pass over through him, with him, and in him.

Therefore, we find the concept of the sacred *voyage* to be a useful image in Catholic spirituality as we "walk" with Christ. As disciples, we are not yet "the saved," but rather "the voyagers" who must travel forward in faith and hope. Before the earliest disciples referred to the "Church Catholic" or even named themselves as the "Christians," they called their Church "the Way."

Our Church over the centuries has endorsed pilgrimage as beneficial for our spirituality. In ancient times, Irish monks spent their whole lives on actual pilgrimage, as they dramatized their hunger for God's presence. More often, European monks remained stably within their monasteries, but they voyaged spiritually to the center of their hearts in search of God. The great cathedrals often designed labyrinths in their vestibules so that people too poor to travel could still walk their pilgrimage symbolically. In our times, Catholics commonly journey to the Holy Land, Rome, Lourdes, Fatima, Guadalupe, and other centers of memorial and devotion.

Our bishops in their constitution on the Church from Vatican Council II have raised our self-consciousness as "a pilgrim Church." Moreover, we celebrate our spiritual voyage ritually in the Holy Eucharist and in all our Sacraments and sacramentals. We annually reenact the rhythm of salvation history by our observance of the liturgical year.

As we voyage, we continuously die and rise in Our Lord who is truly present to accompany us. We can call upon Christ and we can communicate with him, we can cling to Christ and we can depend upon him. Christ encourages us as we deny ourselves, take up our cross, and follow him from egocentricity to Christocentricity. Christ empowers us with his Holy Spirit, lest we fall short in our weakness. He guides us with his Word, lest we become lost in our loneliness. Christ nourishes us with his Sacraments, lest we grow faint in our poverty.

We pursue our spiritual voyage not once and for all, but gradually through a lifetime, not through the spectacular but through the ordinary and the commonplace, so that salvation history becomes our own personal history. Sometimes we confront vicissitudes on our voyage and sometimes we make mistakes. From time to time we may "retreat" from secular concerns to enjoy peaceful moments of healing reform and joyful renewal.

It is a challenge for all of us to persevere on our voyage over the long haul. Monastic wisdom speaks of *acedia*, "the noonday devil," that tempts the monks to go back to bed after lunch instead of returning to their labors. By graced will power, however, we can overcome this demon and energetically persevere on our journey.

As Catholics on voyage, we must embrace several paradoxical factors along our journey. The Risen Christ dwells within us during our voyage, yet he also leads us from out in front. Christ's Spirit purifies us from our human sinfulness, but he also transforms us in divine holiness. We find our nourishment in our Church's scriptures, but we also find our roots in our Church's Tradition. We enjoy Christ's companionship through both Word and Sacrament, we live in "the now" with our vision upon the not-yet, and we observe Christ's law of love with the freedom of God's children.

In this chapter we shall consider the Christian voyage from three perspectives: (1) our asceticism and Christ's Paschal Mystery, (2) our suffering and the Cross of Jesus, and (3) our conversionist rhythm of growth.

Our Asceticism and Christ's Paschal Mystery

Moderate asceticism has always been a critical component of the Christian voyage. *Asceticism* involves self-denial, however, and the very word is overladen with negative connotations. It suggests fasting and sleep-deprivation, and we feel intimidated. It implies impulse-constraint and delayed gratification, and we feel sorry for ourselves. Asceticism requires that we discipline our passions in the interests of civility and channel our instincts in favor of self-control, serenity, and compassion.

Our word "asceticism" comes from the Greek word *asketikos*, which means "trained" or "exercised." "Ascetics" were originally athletes who devoted themselves to physical training for the sake of victory in the games. Christian ascetics of antiquity were the monks and nuns who rigorously disciplined themselves in preparation for transformation by grace.

Our principal motive for asceticism is denial of self according to our Lord's own counsel. We may be reluctant to hear it, but Christ clearly made self-denial a necessary condition for discipleship: "Then he said to them all, 'If any want to become my followers, let them deny themselves and take up their cross daily and follow me. For those who want to save their life will lose it, and those who lose their life for my sake will save it'" (Luke 9:23–24). We die to our former selves in order to live as new selves in Christ. We take up our cross daily in order to rise in Christ. We work to overcome self-centeredness in order to become Christ-centered.

In our Catholic Tradition, certain "spiritual exercises" punctuate our voyage in Christ. We pray privately and liturgically, we fast, and we give alms in our pursuit of personal growth, moderate self-control, and necessary penance for our transgressions. Sometimes, of course, we find it too difficult to deny ourselves, and we hold back. The way of the cross can be bitter, and we shrink from its taste.

By Christ's grace, however, we can recover our vision and commit ourselves once again to the foolishness of Christ's wisdom. We should defer to others before ourselves. We should lend, not expecting payment in return. We should deliver more than others ask for. We should take the last place rather than the first at table. We should give rather than receive, humble rather than exalt ourselves, lose rather than keep our life. The truth of Christ's wisdom is always the same; we can find self-fulfillment only through selflessness. We are in training to become persons of *Agape*-love for God and for one another.

We are bound to love ourselves, of course, since God has loved us first. Authentic love of self, however, demands asceticism, because we tend to love ourselves excessively and preferentially. We are inclined to be self-interested and self-serving, self-indulgent and self-aggrandizing, self-righteous and self-important—the center of the universe. Our tendency to inordinate self-love remains with us through our whole life, and we must vigilantly resist it. Unchecked self-love becomes a narcissistic obsession, inflated with conceit, arrogance, and even hostility toward others. Undisciplined self-love becomes our own short circuit, a sheer vanity that cannot deliver the happiness it promises.

Our Lord calls us to asceticism through union with himself. He invites us to come to him, because he offers us refreshment and rest from our labors. He exhorts us to learn of him, because he is meek and humble of heart. He encourages us to assume his yoke, because it is wondrously light and his grace is sufficient for us.

In Catholic spirituality, therefore, voluntary asceticism is a positive value, a constructive component in the path of Christian discipleship. We must ensure that our asceticism is firm but not rigid so that we may channel our passions with composure, direct our instincts with serenity, and mollify our sharp edges with resiliency. Our asceticism should be humble and not judgmental as we review our own weaknesses. Our asceticism should be forgiving and not harsh as we relate lovingly to our family, friends, and associates.

Christian asceticism energizes our pursuit of personal wholeness. It fortifies us against impulsive, ill-advised ventures, and it protects us from knee-jerk responses to problems. Asceticism tames our minds that we may focus upon life's deepest significance. It purifies our hearts with just motives and noble aspirations. It provides us with virtuous habits that facilitate our right action.

After critical self-reflection, we can diagnose the areas of our lives that require correction or moderation. Asceticism offers a path to liberation from whatever keeps us unfree. We may need to manage our time and prioritize our various tasks more efficiently. We may have to renew our overall motivation; perhaps repetitious, mechanical functions have dulled our enthusiasm, deadened our creativity, and suffocated our initiative. We may discover that we have been self-indulgent in our diversions—perhaps consuming too much time in watching television, attending sports events, or pampering our bodies.

Asceticism enables us to recognize our limitations and humbly claim them as our own. Within discipline's parameters, we can be free to grow in our discipleship. We can determine our goals, we can incorporate our ideals, and we can cultivate our companions for the journey. Such asceticism enables us to order our lives, create our own future, and remain faithful.

We need to control our feelings, since interior peace and unruly sentiments are mutually exclusive. We must subject our emotions to reason and faith, since disorderly passions obstruct enlightenment and altruistic love. We need to discipline our memory, since recollection of imprudent judgments and foolish decisions can jar our serenity. Seven deadly (or "capital") sins can undermine our discipleship: gluttony, greed, lust, anger, pride, envy, and laziness (*acedia* again). Each of these failings stems from a passion unchecked.

Our Suffering and the Cross of Jesus

The "cruel absurdity of human suffering" is by far the most common reason that atheists and agnostics offer for their disbelief in God. How, they argue, can an all-wise, all-good, and all-powerful God exist, when innocent human beings must so often endure pain? Human suffering of mind, heart, and body is a profound mystery for us also, but we may still find meaning and not absurdity through faith in the redemptive Cross of Jesus.

God allows human suffering, we insist, only because God is wise enough, good enough, and powerful enough somehow to draw greater good from it. More often than not, we ourselves cannot perceive this "greater good." Nevertheless, presented with the option of faith or agnosticism, we choose to believe in a God of infinite love. This is our deliberate option, and our spiritual resources enable us to deal with our crosses large and small along the way.

Many of us find that our heaviest cross is utterly to depend upon the caring service of others, but we may for that reason foster a more grateful heart. We may become immobilized, flat on our back in bed and out of commission physically, but we may for that reason grow spiritually through reflection, meditation, and prayerful communion with our Lord.

Our suffering may be physical, like the pain of a headache, a bruise, or a disease. Our suffering may be psychic, like the pain of sore disappointment, hurtful memory, or heartbreaking rejection. Our suffering may be spiritual, like the pain of persistent temptation, oppressive guilt for past sins, or inability to pray. In no case, however, should we squander our suffering to no purpose. As the saying goes, we can "offer it up" in union with Jesus on the Cross. The *Morning Offering* begins with the words, "O Jesus, I offer you my prayers, works, and *sufferings* of this day...."

When we become critically ill, Christ, our divine physician, comes to heal us sacramentally in the anointing of the sick. Anointed people constitute a special "order" in the Church. Christ comes to give us purpose in the very midst of our suffering and to consecrate us in view of his Resurrection. Our lives receive privileged meaning as Christ gives us a special mission toward his kingdom. Whatever our disability, then, we can unite it with the sufferings of Christ for the salvation of the world. Of course, Christ is our Savior, and his redemptive work is already optimal. In God's universal plan, nevertheless, our sufferings in union with Christ can assist in the distribution and application of saving grace to others.

Finally, of course, each of us must die, and nonbelievers

may regard death as the worst of evils and the ultimate absurdity—a dead end, a descent into the dark and bottomless abyss, our final termination. In Catholic spirituality, however, we learn early to pray for the grace of a "happy death," that is, final perseverance in God's grace and friendship.

When death approaches, we send for a priest, who hears our confession and gives us Holy Communion, which at this critical juncture is called *Viaticum* (a Latin word meaning "provision for a journey"). We have hoped in Christ during life, and he has remained within us; we now hope in Christ while dying, and he accompanies us through the veil of death into unimaginable life.

Our Conversionist Rhythm of Growth

Our Catholic spirituality is conversionist. Sometimes we grow and make progress in Christ, but many times during life we fall short and must rise again. Our journey is not simple and beeline, but spiraling—sometimes labyrinthine. We have been called and sanctified, yet we must always acknowledge our sinfulness and seek renewed forgiveness. In the very face of our infidelities, we resolve upon greater fidelity to our vocation. We determine once again, despite our failings, to lead lives of devoted faith, courageous hope, and Christian love.

Within Catholicism, salvation is a goal still to be attained, and we must daily meet challenges old and new in our lifelong voyage. After all, recognizing the need for renewal and reform has always been a factor in Catholic spirituality. We can discern an insistent call to a new conversion. As Vatican Council II put it (quoting from the sixteenth-century Protestant reformers), *"Ecclesia reformata semper reformanda est"* (the reformed Church must always be reformed).

At our baptism, we determine to be Christ's disciples and to live in him as God's adopted sons and daughters. We engage ourselves with God's New Covenant in Christ for the open-ended future so far as we can control it. We regularly renew that commitment through our prayer life and especially through our participation in the Holy Eucharist. We seek to grow as God's children in terms of Christ, our Lord and Savior, the way of the Gospel, and the communion of the holy Church.

> *How far you go in life depends on your being tender with the young, compassionate with the aged, sympathetic with the striving, and tolerant of the weak and strong. Because someday in life you will have been all of these.* (George Washington Carver)

Toward Reflective Journaling

Faithful discipleship according to Christ's mind and heart requires that we understand our extended lives as a process of gradual growth or development into loving children of the Father in the Son.

QUESTIONS FOR DISCUSSION

1. Can you look back upon your life and discern the major junctures of your spiritual voyage in Christ to the Father?

2. Is the metaphor of "spiritual voyage" a source of energizing hope for you as you hear our Lord's insistent call from up ahead?

BIBLIOGRAPHY

Ackroyd, Peter. *The Life of Thomas More.* New York: Random House, 1999.

Barre, Jean-Luc. *Jacques & Raissa Maritain: Beggars for Heaven.* Translated by Bernad E. Doering. Notre Dame, Indiana: University of Notre Dame Press, 2005.

Burghardt, Walter J. S. J. *Long Have I Loved You: A Theologian Reflects on His Church.* Maryknoll, New York: Orbis Books, 2002.

Chadwick, Henry, Tr. *Saint Augustine Confessions.* New York: Oxford University Press, 1991.

Chittester, Joan, O.S.B. *Wisdom Distilled from the Daily: Living the Rule of St. Benedict Today.* New York: HarperCollins, 1990.

Clarke, John, Tr. O.C.D. *Story of a Soul: The Autobiography of St. Therese of Lisieux.* Washington, D.C.: ICS Publications, 1996.

Cunningham, Lawrence S., and Keith J. Egan. *Christian Spirituality: Themes from the Tradition.* New York: Paulist Press, 1996.

Day, Dorothy. *The Long Loneliness: The Autobiography of Dorothy Day.* San Francisco: Harper & Row, 1952.

Downey, Michael. *Understanding Christian Spirituality*. New York: Paulist Press, 1997.

Ford, Michael. *Wounded Prophet: A Portrait of Henri J. M. Nouwen*. New York: Doubleday, 1999.

Hughes, Kathleen, R.S.C.J. *The Monk's Tale: A Biography of Godfrey Diekmann, O.S.B.* Collegeville, Minnesota: Liturgical Press, 1991.

Norris, Kathleen. *The Cloister Walk*. New York: Riverhead Books, 1996.

Nouwen, Henri J. M. *Can You Drink the Cup?* Notre Dame, Indiana: Ave Maria Press, 1996.

Pennington, M. Basil O.S.O. *Centering Prayer: Renewing an Ancient Christian Prayer Form*. New York: Doubleday, 1982.

Rausch, Thomas P., S.J. *Catholicism in the Third Millennium*. A Michael Glazier Book. Collegeville, Minnesota: Liturgical Press, 2003.

Rohr, Richard, and Joseph Martos. *Why Be Catholic? Understanding Our Experience and Tradition*. Cincinnati: St. Anthony Messenger Press, 1989.

Rupp, Joyce. *The Cup of Our Life: A Guide for Spiritual Growth*. Notre Dame, Indiana: Ave Maria Press, 1997.

Teresa, Mother. *No Greater Love*. Novato, California: New World Library, 1989.